THE BEST OF BRIDGE PRESENTS

A YEAR OF THE BEST

SEASONAL RECIPES FROM THE BEST OF BRIDGE
WITH CHEF VINCENT PARKINSON

FIRST PRINTING
July 2001

Copyright© 2001
by The Best of Bridge Publishing Ltd.
FAX: 403-252-0206
EMAIL: order@bestofbridge.com
WEBSITE: www.bestofbridge.com

CANADIAN CATALOGUING IN PUBLICATION DATA

Main entry under title:

"A year of the best"

Includes index.
ISBN 0-9690425-8-2

1. Cookery   I. Brimacombe, Karen.   II. Parkinson, Vincent.
TX715.6.Y42   2001   641.5   C2001-911071-5

Design by:
KARO
Calgary, Alberta

Photography by:
Bilodeau/Preston
Calgary, Alberta

Printed in Canada by:
Centax Books, a Division of PrintWest
1150 Eighth Avenue, Regina, Saskatchewan
Canada S4R 1C9

Oh boy! It's 25 years since the first Best of Bridge cookbook! We're still tasting, testing and publishing—we love this job! Our approach to cooking remains the same: "simple recipes with gourmet results." But it's time for a fresh approach to publishing—and you're holding it! • While we were filming our television series for WTN, we asked Chef Vincent Parkinson, formerly captain of Culinary Team Alberta and Culinary Team Canada, and currently the Chief Executive Chef of the Calgary Golf and Country Club, to join us and demystify the art of carving a turkey. We liked his twinkly smile, his dry sense of humour, and his approach to cooking. So we thought to ourselves: Wouldn't it be fun to do a book with him? We could learn lots of new culinary skills and develop a real home-cooked approach to his gourmet creations. • It was an exciting project. We found Chef Vincent was gracious, helpful, tolerant, and twinkly! We questioned, we cooked, we laughed and we learned! As the book evolved, we realized we were discovering new ways to celebrate the foods of the seasons. We've enjoyed the culinary adventure and we know you'll enjoy the results! Here's to "A Year of the Best!"

KAREN BRIMACOMBE, HELEN MILES, CHEF VINCENT PARKINSON, LINDA JACOBSON, VAL ROBINSON, MARY HALPEN & JOAN WILSON

SPRING

*The true rites of spring
...the first robin...
optimistic tulips pushing
through late snow...the
euphoric scent of lilac
blossoms...buying that
first packet of seeds
...getting ready to grow.*

ASIAN VEGETABLE ROLLS
WITH DIPPING SAUCE

2 Tbsp. (30 mL) **soy sauce**

1 tsp. (5 mL) **cornstarch**

1 tsp. (5 mL) **sugar**

1/2 tsp. (2 mL) **sesame oil**

1/4 tsp. (1 mL) **pepper**

1 Tbsp. (15 mL) **butter**

2 tsp. (10 mL) **freshly grated gingerroot**

1 1/2 cups (375 mL) **chopped fresh shiitake or cremini mushrooms**

1 cup (250 mL) **shredded carrot**

1/2 cup (125 mL) **thinly sliced green onion**

1/4 cup (60 mL) **chopped cilantro**

4 cups (1 L) **finely shredded suey choy (or Napa cabbage), white core removed**

1/3 cup (75 mL) **coarsely chopped salted peanuts**

6–8 sheets phyllo pastry, thawed according to directions

1/3 cup (75 mL) **melted butter**

Dipping Sauce:

juice of 2 limes
3 Tbsp. (45 mL)

3 Tbsp. (45 mL) **rice vinegar**

3 Tbsp. (45 mL) **sesame oil**

1 Tbsp. (15 mL) **liquid honey**

1 Tbsp. (15 mL) **grated gingerroot**

2 garlic cloves, minced

3/4 cup (175 mL) **hoisin sauce**

1 Tbsp. (15 mL) **chopped cilantro**

Very fresh!
Great crunch!
Tangy sauce!
Make ahead;
freeze and cook the
day of your party.

Stir soy, cornstarch, sugar, sesame oil and pepper together in bowl. Set aside.

In large frying pan, stir-fry ginger in butter for about 15 seconds. Add mushrooms, carrot, onion and cilantro to frying pan and stir-fry for 2 minutes. Stir soy mixture and add to vegetables. Mixture will thicken immediately.

Stir cabbage and peanuts into vegetable mixture and remove from heat. Set aside to cool.

Lay one sheet of phyllo vertically on counter and brush bottom half with butter. Fold top half down and press down so it sticks together. Spoon vegetable mixture across short end of the phyllo, forming a 1 1/2" (4 cm) roll. Carefully roll phyllo tightly around mixture folding in the sides as you go. Seal with small amount of melted butter. Place on a cookie sheet, sealed side down. Brush top lightly with butter and score on diagonal (not too deep) about 1" (2.5 cm) apart. Continue with remaining sheets and mixture. At this point, you can wrap each roll in plastic wrap and freeze on a cookie sheet. Keeps up to 2 weeks. Bake at 375°F (190°C) for 15 minutes. Cool slightly and cut at scored intervals. Trim brown ends. Makes 3 dozen.

Combine dipping sauce ingredients in blender. Pour into serving bowl and stir in cilantro. Refrigerate until needed.

CARAMELIZED ONION DIP

1 large yellow onion

¹/₄ **cup** (60 mL) **vegetable oil**

¹/₄ **cup** (60 mL) **butter**

¹/₄ **tsp.** (1 mL) **cayenne pepper**

1 tsp. (5 mL) **salt**

¹/₂ **tsp.** (2 mL) **ground pepper**

4 oz. (115 g) **cream cheese, room temperature**

¹/₂ **cup** (125 mL) **sour cream**

¹/₂ **cup** (125 mL) **mayonnaise**

Cut onion in half and slice thinly.

Heat oil and butter in large frying pan over medium heat.

Add onion, cayenne, salt and pepper and sauté for 10 minutes. Reduce heat to medium-low and cook, stirring occasionally, for 20 minutes more, until onions are browned and caramelized. Cool.

Beat cheese, sour cream and mayonnaise until smooth. Add onions and mix well.

Serve with potato chips or crackers.

This dip also tastes terrific on a hamburger!

GORGONZOLA BABY POTATO BITES

20 tiny red potatoes

4 oz. (115 g) **cream cheese**

2 oz. (55 g) **Gorgonzola cheese**

¼ cup (60 mL) **bacon bits**

1 Tbsp. (15 mL) **chopped fresh basil**

Boil potatoes in salted water until tender. Cool and slice each potato in half. Trim potato bottoms so they don't tip.

Allow cheeses to reach room temperature. Blend well. Add bacon and basil. Dab a small spoonful of mixture on top of each potato. Set on cookie sheet and bake for 10 minutes at 350°F (180°C).

CHEF'S TIP

Full-bodied red wines and ripe peaches, pears and grapes are also perfect with creamy, pungent Gorgonzola – one of Italy's great cheeses.

CHILLED MINTED SPRING PEA SOUP

3 Tbsp. (45 mL) **butter**

1 small onion, chopped

**1 small leek, chopped
(white part only)**

1 celery stalk, chopped

1 garlic clove, minced

3 cups (750 mL) **petite peas
(fresh or frozen)**

4 cups (1 L) **chicken stock**

1¹/₂ Tbsp. (25 mL)
chopped mint

³/₄ cup (175 mL)
light cream

salt and pepper to taste

6 sprigs mint

Melt butter in large saucepan. Add onion, leek and celery and sauté until softened (do not brown). Add garlic and gently sauté for 2 minutes.

Add peas, chicken stock and mint to pan and bring to a boil. Reduce heat and simmer about 10 minutes, until peas are tender. In blender, purée soup in small batches. Strain through sieve.

Stir in cream, chill. Season with salt and pepper. Serve in cold soup plates and garnish with mint.

Oh, the joys of spring – this is one of them!
Serves 6.

SMILE

*The perfect age for
a child: too old for diapers and
too young to drive.*

PEAR AND WATERCRESS SOUP

3 Tbsp. (45 mL) **butter**

**2 medium potatoes,
peeled and cubed**

4 green onions, sliced

14 oz. (398 mL) **can pears,
drained and coarsely
chopped, reserve juice**

2 tsp. (10 mL) **grated
lemon zest**

1/2 tsp. (2 mL)
dried tarragon

2 cups (500 mL) **chicken
or vegetable stock**

**1 bunch watercress, coarsely
chopped, ends removed**

1/2 cup (125 mL) **light cream**

**salt and freshly
ground pepper**

**watercress or green onions,
finely slivered**

In saucepan over medium heat, melt butter gently. Add potatoes and cook for 5-8 minutes, stirring frequently.

———————

Add green onions, pears, lemon zest and tarragon. Stir, cover, and simmer for 3-5 minutes.

———————

Carefully pour in stock and reserved pear juice. Bring soup just to a boil and add watercress. Cover and reduce heat. Simmer until potatoes are tender and watercress is slightly wilted. Remove soup from heat. Purée soup in blender in small batches.

———————

Return soup to saucepan and slowly stir in cream. Heat over medium-low heat until warmed through. Season with salt and pepper.

———————

Garnish soup with watercress or green onions.

———————

*This wonderful soup can be served either hot or cold.
Serves 4-6.*

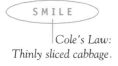

NAPA CABBAGE SALAD

**1 large Napa cabbage,
(suey choy), chopped**

**2 bunches green onions,
chopped**

**1 red bell pepper,
seeded and diced**

1/4 **cup** (60 mL) **butter**

1 cup (250 mL)
slivered almonds

**2 pkgs. chicken-flavoured
oriental soup noodles
with seasoning mix**

Dressing:

1 cup (250 mL) **vegetable oil**

1/2 **cup** (125 mL)
red wine vinegar

2 garlic cloves, minced

2 tsp. (10 mL) **soy sauce**

1/3 **cup** (75 mL) **sugar**

Place chopped cabbage, green onions and red pepper in large salad bowl.

Melt butter in frying pan and sauté almonds, broken noodles and seasonings until golden. Add to cabbage mixture and toss.

Shake dressing ingredients in a jar. Pour over salad and toss at least 1/2 hour before serving. You will have extra dressing, refrigerate and use again.

Excellent for picnics, buffets – and teenagers!
Serves 10-12.

MARINATED VEGETABLE SALAD WITH DIJON DRESSING

1 cup (250 mL) **cauliflower florets**

1 cup (250 mL) **broccoli florets**

¹/₂ lb. (250 g) **green beans, trimmed**

¹/₂ red pepper, sliced in strips

14 oz. (398 mL) **can hearts of palm, drained and cut into ¹/₂"** (1.5 cm) **pieces**

Dijon Dressing:

¹/₃ cup (75 mL) **olive oil**

3 Tbsp. (45 mL) **red wine vinegar**

1 Tbsp. (15 mL) **Dijon mustard**

¹/₄ tsp. (1 mL) **salt**

freshly ground pepper

¹/₄ tsp. (1 mL) **dried oregano**

small garlic clove, minced

Add cauliflower and broccoli florets to boiling water. Boil 2-3 minutes. Remove with slotted spoon. Rinse under cold water and drain.

———————

Return water to boil and add green beans. Boil 2 minutes. Drain and rinse with cold water.

———————

Combine cauliflower, broccoli, green beans, red pepper and hearts of palm in a large bowl.

———————

Whisk dressing ingredients together and pour over vegetables. Toss to mix. Cover and refrigerate 2-3 hours before serving.

———————

Serves 4.

AVOCADO AND GRAPEFRUIT SALAD WITH LIME VINAIGRETTE

Lime Vinaigrette:

¼ **cup** (60 mL) **freshly squeezed lime juice**

1 **Tbsp.** (15 mL) **liquid honey**

¼ **tsp.** (1 mL) **crushed red pepper flakes**

¼ **tsp.** (1 mL) **dry mustard**

¼ **cup** (60 mL) **sugar**

½ **cup** (125 mL) **vegetable oil**

salt and freshly ground pepper

1 **head red leaf lettuce**

2 **avocados, sliced into** 1" (2.5 cm) **pieces**

1 **large red grapefruit, peeled and pith removed, sliced crosswise into** ¼" (0.5 cm) **pieces**

Pour lime juice and honey in blender and add pepper flakes, dry mustard and sugar. Whirl. Slowly pour in oil and whirl until thoroughly blended. Add salt and pepper to taste. Set aside in refrigerator until ready to use.

Place salad ingredients in salad bowl. Toss with vinaigrette just before serving.

Great with fish or fowl.
Serves 6-8.

PASTA WITH TOMATO SALSA AND FETA

6 fresh tomatoes

1/4 cup (60 mL) **fresh Parmesan cheese, shaved into ribbons**

2 cups (500 mL) **torn fresh spinach**

1 garlic clove, minced

1/3 cup (75 mL) **olive oil**

1/2 cup (125 mL) **chopped fresh basil**

freshly ground pepper to taste

1 lb. (500 g) **penne**

1/2 cup (125 mL) **crumbled feta cheese**

3 Tbsp. (45 mL) **pine nuts, toasted**

2 Tbsp. (30 mL) **chopped fresh parsley**

Cut an "X" through skin at bottom of each tomato. Blanch tomatoes in boiling water for 30 seconds. Plunge in cold water and peel off skin with sharp knife. Cut in half and remove seeds. Coarsely chop and set aside in a bowl.

Add Parmesan, spinach, garlic, oil, basil and pepper to tomatoes.

Cook penne in boiling salted water until tender. Drain and toss with tomato mixture. Top with feta and pine nuts and sprinkle with parsley.

Serves 6.

SHRIMP CAKES WITH JALAPEÑO TARTAR SAUCE

Shrimp Cakes:

¹/₂ **cup** (125 mL) **clam juice or water**

1¹/₂ **lbs.** (750 g) **uncooked shrimp, peeled and deveined**

2 **Tbsp.** (30 mL) **butter**

1 **stalk celery, finely diced**

8 **green onions, sliced**

1¹/₄ **cups** (310 mL) **finely crushed soda crackers**

1 **tsp.** (5 mL) **hot pepper sauce**

2 **eggs, well beaten**

¹/₃ **cup** (75 mL) **mayonnaise**

¹/₄ **cup** (60 mL) **snipped chives**

salt and freshly ground pepper

3 **cups** (750 mL) **bread crumbs**

2 **Tbsp.** (30 mL) **butter**

Jalapeño Tartar Sauce:

1 **cup** (250 mL) **mayonnaise**

1 **tsp.** (5 mL) **Dijon mustard**

2 **tsp.** (10 mL) **fresh lemon juice**

¹/₄ **cup** (60 mL) **minced gherkin pickles**

1 **fresh jalapeño pepper, seeded and finely chopped**

salt and freshly ground pepper to taste

Serves 6.

In frying pan, bring clam juice to a boil. Add shrimp and reduce heat. Cover and simmer for 2 minutes or until shrimp are pink. Drain and transfer to a bowl. Cool slightly. Finely chop shrimp and set aside.

Over low heat, melt butter and cook celery until soft. Add green onion and cook until soft, stirring occasionally.

To chopped shrimp add soda crackers, hot pepper sauce, eggs, mayonnaise, chives and seasonings. Add to celery mixture. Shape into 12 cakes. If mixture doesn't hold its shape, add about ¹/₂ cup (125 mL) breadcrumbs.

Spread crumbs (less if you used some in shrimp mixture) in shallow bowl and dredge cakes in them, coating evenly. Melt butter over medium heat and sauté half the cakes, turning once, until golden (about 6 minutes total). Keep warm. Sauté remaining cakes, adding more butter if needed.

Blend sauce ingredients together and store in refrigerator.

CHEF'S TIP

Celery root (celeriac) is readily available. Look for a firm piece with green shoots on top. Peel like a potato, and add lemon juice to prevent the white flesh from discolouring. Raw celery root can be grated and added to salads.

WHIPPED POTATO WITH CELERY ROOT

1 celery root, peeled and chopped

4-5 baker potatoes, peeled and cut into chunks

2 Tbsp. (30 mL) **butter**

3 Tbsp. (45 mL) **sour cream**

grated zest of 1 orange

salt and freshly ground pepper to taste

Cook celery root in simmering salted water until tender. Drain and purée in food processor.

Cook potatoes in salted water until tender. Drain and mash, mixing in butter and sour cream.

Add zest to mashed celery root then add to mashed potatoes. Season with salt and pepper.

Celery root does wonders for the humble potato.
Serves 6.

CEDAR PLANK SALMON
WITH CUCUMBER DILL SAUCE

1 untreated cedar plank

2 shallots, diced

10 cloves garlic, minced

3 Tbsp. (45 mL) **snipped fresh dill**

3 Tbsp. (45 mL) **chopped fresh thyme**

2 Tbsp. (30 mL) **chopped fresh cilantro**

2 Tbsp. (30 mL) **grated lemon zest**

3 Tbsp. (45 mL) **fresh lemon juice**

2 green onions, chopped

1 tsp. (5 mL) **olive oil**

3-4 lb. (1.5-2 kg) **salmon fillet**

salt and freshly ground pepper to taste

Cucumber Dill Sauce:

¼ English cucumber

¼ tsp. (1 mL) **salt**

1 cup (250 mL) **plain yogurt**

½ cup (125 mL) **sour cream**

1 tsp. (5 mL) **lemon juice**

pepper to taste

3 green onions, finely chopped, white part only

2 tsp. (10 mL) **chopped fresh dill or 1 tsp.** (5 mL) **dried**

Soak cedar plank in water for several hours.

In small glass bowl, combine shallots, garlic, dill, thyme, cilantro, lemon zest and juice, green onions and olive oil. Cover and place in refrigerator for at least 1 hour to allow flavours to get acquainted.

Place salmon on cedar plank and sprinkle with salt and pepper. Cover with herb mixture. Set plank on barbecue and close lid. Bake for 30 minutes on medium heat, until fish flakes easily with a fork.

To prepare Cucumber Dill Sauce, finely chop cucumber, toss with salt and let stand for 15 minutes.

Combine yogurt, sour cream, lemon juice, pepper, onion and dill.

Drain water from cucumber and add to yogurt mixture.

Serves 8.

CHEF'S TIP

Use pliers to pull out the "pin bones" that run the length of the salmon.

LEMON RISOTTO

1 Tbsp. (15 mL)
olive oil

1½ cups (375 mL) **sliced
shiitake mushrooms**

**2 shallots or green
onions, thinly sliced**

2 garlic cloves, minced

dash of pepper

1 cup (250 mL) **Arborio or
short-grain rice**

2 cups (500 mL)
chicken stock

½ cup (125 mL) **dry
white wine or water**

**1 large carrot cut into
1"** (2.5 cm) **matchsticks**

**1 small bunch asparagus
spears, cut into 1"**
(2.5 cm) **pieces**

¼ cup (60 mL) **freshly
grated Parmesan cheese**

2 tsp. (10 mL) **grated
lemon zest**

**fresh basil or
parsley (optional)**

In large saucepan, heat oil and cook mushrooms, shallots, garlic and pepper until vegetables are tender but not brown.

Add rice and cook and stir 2 minutes more. Stir broth and wine into rice mixture and bring to a boil. Reduce heat, cover and simmer for 30 minutes (do not lift cover). Remove from heat.

Stir in carrots, asparagus, Parmesan and lemon zest. Cover and let stand for 5 minutes. Add a little additional water, if necessary for the desired consistency.

Garnish with basil or parsley.

*This Lemon Risotto recipe transforms simple rice into a wonderful dinner or side dish. Great with Cedar Plank Salmon on page 18.
Serves 8.*

CHICKEN WITH ASPARAGUS AND LEMON-TARRAGON CREAM

4 boneless, skinless chicken breast halves

¹/₂ tsp. (2 mL) salt

¹/₂ tsp. (2 mL) pepper

2 Tbsp. (30 mL) vegetable oil

1 Tbsp. (15 mL) vegetable oil

1 lb. (500 g) asparagus, cut into 3" (7.5 cm) pieces

¹/₄ tsp. (1 mL) salt

³/₄ cup (175 mL) whipping cream

1 Tbsp. (15 mL) chopped fresh tarragon

³/₄ tsp. (3 mL) grated lemon zest

Sprinkle chicken breasts with salt and pepper. Heat 2 Tbsp. (30 mL) oil in frying pan and sauté chicken. Don't overcook! Remove chicken from pan and keep warm.

———

Add oil to frying pan and sauté asparagus with salt until just tender. Remove from pan.

———

Wipe pan clean and add cream, tarragon and lemon zest. Simmer 3-4 minutes, until slightly thickened. Add asparagus to sauce.

———

To serve, place chicken breasts on serving plate, pour sauce with asparagus over chicken and garnish with lemon zest. Serve with rice.

———

Perfect "after-work" fare or Friday night after martinis! Serves 4.

CHEF'S TIP

A rasp is an excellent tool for zesting citrus fruits.

RACK OF LAMB WITH
HERB AND MUSTARD CRUST

2 slices bread

2 Tbsp. (30 mL) **chopped fresh parsley**

1 Tbsp. (15 mL) **chopped fresh rosemary**

2 Tbsp. (30 mL) **chopped fresh basil**

1 garlic clove, minced

2 racks of 8 lamb chops

olive oil

3 Tbsp. (45 mL) **Dijon mustard**

Fresh Mint Pesto:

2 cups (500 mL) **fresh mint**

¼ cup (60 mL) **chopped onion**

¼ cup (60 mL) **lime juice**

2 Tbsp. (30 mL) **white wine vinegar**

2 Tbsp. (30 mL) **sugar**

¼ cup (60 mL) **chopped parsley**

Tear bread into pieces and place in food processor. Add parsley, rosemary, basil and garlic. Pulse to make fine crumb mixture.

Heat oil in heavy-bottomed frying pan and sear lamb on all sides. This can also be done on barbecue.

Brush mustard over lamb, then press into crumb mixture. This can be done ahead of time.

Preheat oven to 400°F (200°C). Roast for 20-30 minutes for medium-rare.

Remove from oven and rest lamb for 5 minutes before carving into chops.

To prepare Fresh Mint Pesto, combine ingredients in blender or small food processor and purée.

Chill and serve with lamb.

Allow 4 chops per person.
Serves 4.

RACK OF LAMB WITH BLACK OLIVE PASTE

³/₄ cup (175 mL) **black olives (Kalamata), pitted**

2-3 anchovies

2 Tbsp. (30 mL) **capers**

1 garlic clove

¹/₄ cup (60 mL) **olive oil**

3 Tbsp. (45 mL) **Dijon mustard**

3 Tbsp. (45 mL) **Parmesan cheese**

¹/₂ cup (125 mL) **fresh breadcrumbs**

1 tsp. (5 mL) **chopped fresh basil**

3 racks of 8 lamb chops

2 Tbsp. (30 mL) **canola oil**

Purée olives, anchovies, capers and garlic in food processor. With food processor running, add olive oil to make a smooth paste. Stir mustard into olive paste.

Mix Parmesan, breadcrumbs and basil together. Set aside.

Sear lamb in hot oil, browning all sides.

Spread each rack of lamb with olive paste, and then dip into crumb mixture.

Preheat oven to 400°F (200°C). Roast 20-30 minutes for medium-rare. Rest racks 5 minutes before carving.

Serves 6.

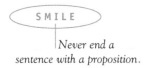
SPICY ORANGE CHICKEN STIR-FRY

**4 boneless, skinless
chicken breast halves**

1 Tbsp. (15 mL) soy sauce

1 Tbsp. (15 mL) dry sherry

1 Tbsp. (15 mL) oyster sauce

2 tsp. (10 mL) orange zest

2 red bell peppers

1 small zucchini

1 large cooking onion

Spicy Orange Sauce:

juice of 1 orange

¼ cup (60 mL) dry sherry

1 Tbsp. (15 mL) oyster sauce

1 Tbsp. (15 mL) sesame oil

**2-4 tsp. (10-20 mL)
Asian chili sauce**

1 Tbsp. (15 mL) cornstarch

3 Tbsp. (45 mL) cooking oil

4 garlic cloves, minced

**1" (2.5 cm) piece
fresh gingerroot, peeled
and chopped**

Cut chicken into ½" (1.5 cm) cubes. Combine soy sauce, sherry, oyster sauce and orange zest. Mix with chicken and marinate 15 minutes at room temperature.

Seed and stem peppers. Cut into ½" (1.5 cm) cubes. Cut zucchini lengthwise (don't peel) into 4 strips. Cut each strip crosswise into ½" (1.5 cm) pieces. Peel onion and cut into thin wedges. Cut each wedge in half. Combine veggies in bowl.

You're probably wondering why you have to cut everything into uniform sizes!
Not only do the ingredients cook evenly, they look carefully considered. Very Zen!

To prepare Spicy Orange Sauce, combine orange juice, sherry, oyster sauce, sesame oil, chili sauce and cornstarch in small bowl. Set aside.

Place wok or heavy frying pan over high heat. When wok becomes hot, add 2 Tbsp. (30 mL) oil. When oil smokes, add chicken and stir 2 minutes. Remove to plate. Add remaining 1 Tbsp. (15 mL) of oil along with garlic and gingerroot. Stir for 5 seconds. Add veggies and stir 2 minutes. Add Spicy Orange Sauce and chicken and stir until sauce thickens. Serve immediately with steamed rice.

We like the simplicity of this recipe – and the orange flavour!
Serves 4.

PATIO RIBS

4 lbs. (2 kg) **(3-4 racks)**
pork back spareribs

½ cup (125 mL)
hoisin sauce

½ cup (125 mL)
oyster sauce

3 Tbsp. (45 mL)
hot chili sauce

2 Tbsp. (30 mL)
liquid honey

Remove skin from underside of ribs (see chef's tip). To tenderize ribs, slice each rack in half and add to large pot of boiling water. Boil gently until ribs are fork-tender (45 minutes). Drain.

Stir hoisin, oyster, hot chili sauce and honey together.

Generously coat ribs with sauce on each side. When ready to barbecue, spray grill with oil and cook over medium heat, basting with sauce and turning often until well glazed, about 15 minutes.

Sticky ribs – "Dee-rishus Gramma!"
Also great as an appetizer.
Serves 4.

CHEF'S TIP

To remove "fell" (tough membrane that covers bony underside of ribs), place ribs meaty-side down on a flat surface. Using point of a knife or your fingers, loosen skin and pull back along end of last rib. Grasp membrane with a paper towel or pliers and peel away. Discard.

BREAD AND BUTTER PUDDING WITH RHUBARB COULIS

Custard:

1 cup (250 mL) **evaporated milk**

1 cup (250 mL) **whipping cream**

1 Tbsp. (15 mL) **vanilla**

2 eggs

¹/₂ cup (125 mL) **sugar**

pinch salt

Pudding:

4 large slices French bread or enough bread to fill baking dish

butter

cinnamon

Rhubarb Coulis:

2 cups (500 mL) **chopped rhubarb (frozen is fine)**

¹/₂ cup (125 mL) **sugar**

¹/₄ cup (60 mL) **water**

juice of ¹/₂ lemon

To prepare custard, combine evaporated milk, whipping cream and vanilla in saucepan and heat to a boil.

Whisk eggs, sugar and salt together and add to boiling milk. Strain through sieve.

Butter an 8x8" (20x20 cm) baking dish. Butter bread and cut into 1" (2.5 cm) pieces. Fill the dish with bread and generously dust with cinnamon.

Pour custard over bread, ensuring all pieces underneath become moist. Soak for 30 minutes. Place dish in pan of hot water 2" (5 cm) deep. Bake at 350°F (180°C) for 35-40 minutes, or until custard is set and pudding is golden brown.

To make coulis, combine rhubarb, sugar, water and lemon juice in saucepan. Simmer until rhubarb is tender, then purée in blender.

Spoon warm pudding onto individual plates and top with Rhubarb Coulis.

Serves 8.

CHEF'S TIP

Make smaller
biscuits to serve with dinner.

SHORTCAKE BISCUITS WITH LEMON CREAM AND STRAWBERRIES

Biscuits:

3 cups (750 mL) **flour**

1 Tbsp. (15 mL) **sugar**

1 Tbsp. (15 mL)
baking powder

2 tsp. (10 mL)
cream of tartar

1 tsp. (5 mL) **baking soda**

1 tsp. (5 mL) **salt**

³/₄ cup (175 mL)
chilled butter

1¹/₄ cups (310 mL)
light cream

Lemon Cream Filling:

2 eggs

2 Tbsp. (30 mL) **butter**

1 cup (250 mL) **sugar**

juice of 2 lemons

grated lemon zest

1 cup (250 mL)
whipping cream

strawberries, sliced

Combine dry ingredients in a large bowl.

Cut in butter with pastry blender until mixture resembles coarse meal.

Add cream, stirring with fork. Shape dough into ball and knead on floured surface 8 times. Roll out into a 1" (2.5 cm) thick rectangle. Cut into 8 squares or, if you prefer round biscuits, use a 3" (7.5 cm) biscuit cutter. Place on baking sheet and bake for 10-12 minutes at 425°F (220°C). Biscuits should be golden brown.

To make filling, combine eggs, butter, sugar, juice and zest in saucepan and bring to a boil. Reduce heat and cook, stirring constantly, for 15 minutes. Cover and cool in refrigerator.

Whip cream and fold gently into lemon mixture.

To serve, cut biscuits in half and fill with lemon cream and strawberries. Replace top.

The best baking powder biscuits we've ever made!
Serves 8.

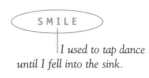
MERINGUE COOKIES

1 cup (250 mL)
toasted sliced almonds

2 egg whites

¼ tsp. (1 mL)
cream of tartar

1 cup (250 mL) **berry sugar**

1 tsp. (5 mL) **almond**
or vanilla extract

To toast almonds, spread on baking sheet and bake at 350°F (180°C) for 5 minutes. Watch carefully! Cool.

Beat egg whites and cream of tartar until light and fluffy.

Gradually add sugar to egg white mixture and continue beating until mixture stands in stiff peaks. Gently fold almonds into meringue with almond extract.

Drop meringue by teaspoonsful onto lightly greased baking sheet. Bake at 300°F (150°C) for 30 minutes.

For afternoon tea or to celebrate holidays and new grandchildren.
Makes about 48 cookies.

LEMON PISTACHIO SNAPS

2 cups (500 mL) **flour**

1/2 tsp. (2 mL) **baking soda**

1/4 tsp. (1 mL) **salt**

3/4 cup (175 mL) **butter, softened**

3/4 cup (175 mL) **berry sugar**

1 large egg

1 Tbsp. (15 mL) **grated lemon zest**

1 Tbsp. (15 mL) **fresh lemon juice**

1/3 cup (75 mL) **finely chopped pistachio nuts**

3 Tbsp. (45 mL) **sugar**

In large bowl, mix together flour, baking soda and salt.

Using a mixer, cream together butter and sugar until light and fluffy. Beat in egg, mixing until just combined. Add lemon zest and lemon juice. Blend in dry ingredients and combine thoroughly. Wrap dough in plastic wrap and chill for 1 hour.

In small bowl, combine pistachio nuts and sugar. Shape dough into 1" (2.5 cm) balls. Roll balls in pistachio sugar mixture. Place 2" (5 cm) apart on greased baking sheets. Press cookies down with small glass to flatten slightly. Bake at 350°F (180°C) for 10-12 minutes, until golden. Transfer to racks to cool.

Makes 5 dozen cookies.

SUMMER

Jumping through the sprinkler is just as much fun when you're an adult. There is no sweeter sound than ice cubes clinking in a glass. And soaking up a long summer afternoon is enough to replenish your soul.

CORNMEAL CURRANT GRIDDLE CAKES WITH APPLE CINNAMON SYRUP

Syrup:

2 cups (500 mL) **apple juice**

1/2 cup (125 mL) **apple jelly**

3″ (7.5 cm)
cinnamon stick

Griddle Cakes:

1 cup (250 mL) **flour**

1/2 cup (125 mL) **cornmeal**

3 Tbsp. (45 mL) **sugar**

2 tsp. (10 mL) **baking powder**

1 tsp. (5 mL) **baking soda**

pinch of salt

1/3 cup (75 mL) **currants**

1 1/4 cups (310 mL)
plain yogurt

2 large eggs

1/4 cup (60 mL)
melted butter

Put syrup ingredients in medium-sized saucepan and gently boil over medium-high heat for 20 minutes (watch carefully last 5 minutes). Reduce to 1 cup (250 mL).

To make griddle cakes, combine flour, cornmeal, sugar, baking powder, baking soda and salt in large bowl.

Stir currants into flour mixture.

Mix yogurt and eggs in small bowl and stir into flour mixture. This is a very thick batter.

Stir in butter.

Heat lightly greased frying pan or griddle over low heat until hot. Pour batter in batches forming 3″ (7.5 cm) cakes. Cook about 3 minutes on one side or until bubbles form and bottom is golden. Turn and cook other side until golden. Keep warm while cooking remaining cakes. Serve with warm syrup.

Cornmeal and currants – you've gotta try this!
Serves 4.

CALIFORNIA ROLLS

2 cups (500 mL)
Japanese sushi rice

2 cups (500 mL) **water**

¼ **cup** (60 mL) **rice vinegar**

3 Tbsp. (45 mL) **sugar**

1½ **tsp.** (7 mL) **salt**

1 bamboo sushi mat

4-5 sheets nori

wasabi paste

4 oz. (115 g) **crab meat, shredded or 4 pollock tubes**

1 cucumber, seeded, cut in strips

6 green onions, cut in strips

1 avocado, cut in strips

1 red pepper, cut in strips

wasabi paste

pickled ginger

soy sauce

Place rice in colander and rinse with cold water. Combine rice and water and bring to boil. Cover and cook on low for 15 minutes. Remove from heat and let stand for 10 minutes.

Stir vinegar, sugar and salt together. Transfer rice to bowl and toss with mixture. Set aside to cool.

Place bamboo mat on flat surface with reeds running horizontal to you. Place a nori sheet (smooth side down) on mat. Dampen your fingers and press 1 cup (250 mL) of rice to cover nori leaving 1" (2.5 cm) edge on top and bottom but pressing all the way to sides.

Spread thin line of wasabi on lower edge of rice. Place strip of seafood along the wasabi, then cucumber, green onion, avocado and red pepper strips. Using mat as a support, roll nori over filling. Press tightly with fingers and continue rolling nori. Moisten top edge of nori with water to seal roll. Trim ends and keep refrigerated under damp towel until ready to serve.

To serve, slice into 1" (2.5 cm) pieces and place on platter. Serve with extra wasabi, pickled ginger and soy sauce.

Chef taught us, "practice makes perfect."
Makes 32 pieces.

SALAD ROLLS

1 pkg. rice vermicelli noodles

suey choy, shredded

fresh mint leaves, chopped

1-2 large carrots, peeled and shredded

bean sprouts

fresh ginger, peeled and grated

green onions, finely chopped

medium shrimp, cooked and cut in half lengthwise

1 pkg. small rice paper rounds

Plunge noodles in boiling water for 2 minutes. Rinse in cold water and drain well. Chop in 2-3" (5-7.5 cm) pieces and set aside.

Prepare suey choy, mint leaves, carrots, bean sprouts, ginger, green onion and shrimp.

Soak rice paper rounds one at a time in hot water until pliable. Place small amount of noodles near bottom of a round but not too near the sides. Place a few strips of suey choy, a sprinkling of mint, carrot, bean sprouts, ginger and green onions, and top with shrimp.

Make one complete roll from the bottom and then fold the sides towards middle. Continue rolling as many as you need and set aside. Wrap rolls individually in plastic wrap. Store in refrigerator until ready to serve.

Make these with a gathering of friends. Serve with dipping sauce – peanut, hoisin or Thai chili sauce.

THAI NOODLE SALAD

Vinaigrette:

¹/₄ **cup** (60 mL)
fresh lime juice

3 **Tbsp.** (45 mL)
vegetable oil

3 **Tbsp.** (45 mL) **soy sauce**

2 **Tbsp.** (30 mL) **brown sugar**

1 **Tbsp.** (15 mL) **sesame oil**

1 **Tbsp.** (15 mL) **minced garlic**

1 **Tbsp.** (15 mL) **grated
orange or lime zest**

1 **Tbsp.** (15 mL)
**minced Anaheim chili
(or use jalapeño pepper
for more heat)**

salt and pepper to taste

¹/₂ **lb.** (250 g) **green beans
or asparagus spears**

8 **oz.** (250 g) **Chinese egg
noodles, fresh or dried**

2 **cups** (500 mL)
peeled, shredded carrots

¹/₂ **cup** (125 mL)
slivered red pepper

1 **cup** (250 mL) **thinly sliced
green onions for garnish**

Whisk vinaigrette ingredients together
and set aside.

Trim green beans or asparagus and cut
diagonally into ¹/₂" (1.5 cm) pieces.
Cook in boiling water until tender crisp.
Plunge into cold water (to retain colour)
and set aside. Drain well.

Cook noodles according to package directions.
Drain well.

Toss noodles with vegetables and vinaigrette.
Cover and refrigerate at least 2 hours or
overnight. Garnish with green onions
before serving.

*Serve with Thai Grilled Chicken on page 54.
Serves 6.*

GRILLED FETA WITH TOMATOES

1 lb. (500 g) **mixture of yellow, green and red tomatoes**

butter lettuce

1 lb. (500 g) **chunk feta cheese**

2 Tbsp. (30 mL) **extra-virgin olive oil**

bunch of fresh basil leaves

¹/₄ cup (60 mL) **extra-virgin olive oil**

freshly ground pepper

Slice tomatoes and arrange on serving plates with lettuce.

Cut feta into 6 even slices and place on lightly oiled cookie sheet. Drizzle with oil and heat under broiler until lightly browned. Place warm feta on top of tomatoes.

Chop basil and sprinkle over salad. Drizzle with oil and sprinkle with freshly ground pepper.

Buy some fresh tomatoes at the farmer's market and create this superb salad. Serves 6.

CHEF'S TIP

To develop the full flavour of tomatoes, do not store in the refrigerator. Keep them on the kitchen counter and enjoy the colour!

MANGO AND SPICY SHRIMP SALAD

Honey-Chive Salad Dressing:

1 egg yolk

2 Tbsp. (30 mL)
white wine vinegar

1 tsp. (5 mL)
fresh lemon juice

1¼ cups (310 mL)
canola oil

3 Tbsp. (45 mL) **snipped fresh chives**

1 Tbsp. (15 mL) **finely chopped fresh parsley**

1 Tbsp. (15 mL) **liquid honey**

1 garlic clove, minced

pinch of salt

Salad:

3 mangoes

1 lime

1 medium jicama

¼ English cucumber

2 radishes

24 large, uncooked shrimp peeled and deveined

1 Tbsp. (15 mL)
Cajun seasoning

1 Tbsp. (15 mL) **vegetable oil**

1 pkg. mixed lettuce

To make Honey-Chive Salad Dressing, whisk egg yolk, gradually adding vinegar and lemon juice. Whisk in canola oil until well incorporated.

Add remaining ingredients, shake well and store in refrigerator.

Peel and slice mango. Squeeze juice from lime and toss with mango.

Peel and slice jicama and cucumber into strips. Thinly slice radishes.

Coat shrimp with Cajun seasoning and quickly pan-fry in oil until just cooked (pink).

Divide lettuce among 6 plates. Arrange mango and vegetables on lettuce. Drizzle with Honey-Chive Dressing and place cooked shrimp on each salad.

Serves 6.

SWEET PEPPER AND SNOW PEA SALAD WITH SOY VINAIGRETTE

Salad:

³/₄ lb. (340 g) snow peas, strings removed

1 red pepper, cut in strips

1 yellow pepper, cut in strips

1 cup (250 mL) fresh bean sprouts

8 water chestnuts, sliced

Soy Vinaigrette:

3 shiitake mushrooms

¹/₄ red pepper

1 shallot

1 garlic clove

¹/₂ tsp. (2 mL) minced fresh ginger

3 Tbsp. (45 mL) rice vinegar

2¹/₂ Tbsp. (35 mL) soy sauce

2 tsp. (10 mL) sesame oil

¹/₂ cup (125 mL) vegetable oil

1 Tbsp. (15 mL) honey

2 Tbsp. (30 mL) sesame seeds, toasted

Blanch pea pods in boiling water for 2 minutes. Plunge in cold water, drain and pat dry. Place snow peas, peppers, bean sprouts and water chestnuts in salad bowl.

To prepare soy vinaigrette, blanch mushrooms in boiling water for 2 minutes. Plunge in cold water and drain well. In food processor finely chop mushrooms, red pepper, shallot, garlic and ginger.

In small bowl, combine vinegar and soy sauce. Whisk in oils and honey. Add chopped vegetables and whisk together.

Toss prepared salad vegetables with vinaigrette and sprinkle with toasted sesame seeds.

GREEN BEANS WITH RASPBERRY VINAIGRETTE

Raspberry Vinaigrette:

2 Tbsp. (30 mL) **raspberry vinegar**

1/2 tsp. (2 mL) **whole-grain mustard (or Dijon)**

pinch of salt

1 tsp. (5 mL) **honey**

3 Tbsp. (45 mL) **olive oil**

1 garlic clove, minced

1 lb. (500 g) **fresh young green beans, ends snipped**

1 red pepper, cut in strips

3 green onions, thinly sliced

1/4 cup (60 mL) **toasted pine nuts**

Whisk together vinaigrette ingredients.

Blanch beans in salted boiling water for 2 minutes, drain and plunge into ice water. Drain well.

Toss beans, red pepper and onions with vinaigrette. Sprinkle with pine nuts.

Vinaigrette adds kick to crunchy green beans.
Serves 4-6.

CHEF'S TIP

To toast pine nuts, spread on a baking pan and place in a 350°F (180°C) oven for about 5 minutes. Stir during baking. Watch carefully.

MAYAN GRILLED SHRIMP

wooden skewers

2 lbs. (1 kg) **large
shrimp in the shell**

Marinade:

¼ cup (60 mL)
fresh lime juice

¼ cup (60 mL) **tequila**

2 shallots, finely chopped

2 garlic cloves, minced

2 tsp. (10 mL) **ground cumin**

salt and ground pepper

½ cup (125 mL) **olive oil**

Soak skewers in water for at least 30 minutes.

Thread 4 shrimp on each skewer. Lay in single layer in a shallow glass dish.

To make marinade, whisk together lime juice, tequila, shallots, garlic, cumin, and salt and pepper to taste. Slowly add olive oil, whisking until combined. Taste for seasoning.

Pour marinade over shrimp and let marinate for at least 30 minutes, or up to 4 hours in the refrigerator.

Heat barbecue to medium heat. Grill shrimp about 2 minutes on each side, just until pink.

Excellent served as an appetizer or an entrée.
Serves 8.

RIB-EYE STEAKS WITH GRILLED PEPPERS AND GORGONZOLA BUTTER

Gorgonzola Butter:

¹/₄ cup (60 mL) **crumbled Gorgonzola cheese**

2 Tbsp. (30 mL) **butter, room temperature**

1 Tbsp. (15 mL) **minced fresh marjoram or oregano**

pepper to taste

Marinade:

¹/₂ cup (125 mL) **olive oil**

6 large garlic cloves, minced

2 Tbsp. (30 mL) **minced fresh marjoram**

4 x 1" (4 x 2.5 cm) **thick rib-eye steaks**

2 large red bell peppers, cut into 1¹/₂" (4 cm) **strips**

2 large yellow bell peppers, cut into 1¹/₂" (4 cm) **strips**

2 large green bell peppers cut into 1¹/₂" (4 cm) **strips**

salt and freshly ground pepper to taste

In small bowl, beat together Gorgonzola, butter and marjoram. Season with pepper.

Combine oil, garlic and marjoram in shallow glass baking dish.

Place steaks and peppers in marinade. Turn to coat. Let stand 2 hours at room temperature or overnight in refrigerator. Turn occasionally.

Heat barbecue to medium high. Place steaks and peppers on grill. Sprinkle with salt and pepper. Grill steaks 5 minutes per side for medium-rare.

Grill peppers until tender (10 minutes), turning occasionally.

Transfer steaks to platter and surround with peppers. Top each steak with Gorgonzola Butter.

Sensational with Spätzle on page 70.
Serves 4.

TEQUILA SEA BASS

Salsa:

1 tsp. (5 mL) **lime zest**

juice of 2 limes

¼ tsp. (1 mL) **freshly ground pepper**

1½ cups (375 mL) **chopped ripe Roma tomatoes**

½ cup (125 mL) **sliced green onion**

1 Tbsp. (15 mL) **tequila**

2 x 6 oz. (2 x 170 g) **sea bass fillets**

¼ cup (60 mL) **flour**

½ tsp. (2 mL) **salt**

¼ tsp. (1 mL) **freshly ground pepper**

1 Tbsp. (15 mL) **olive oil**

Combine salsa ingredients in small bowl. Cover and refrigerate at least 2 hours.

Using sharp knife, remove skin from fillets. Preheat oven to 350°F (180°C). Combine flour, salt and pepper in shallow bowl and dredge fish in mixture. Heat oil in ovenproof skillet over medium-high heat. Add fish and cook 5 minutes on one side. Turn fish over and top with salsa. Bake at 350°F (180°C) for 15 minutes or just until fish flakes easily. Don't overcook!

Always moist and delicious. Serve with Basmati rice and steamed green beans. A fast dinner for 2.

TIPSY

One tequila,
Two tequila,
Three tequila,
Floor.

THAI GRILLED CHICKEN

Marinade:

¹⁄₃ **cup** (75 mL) **fresh basil**

¹⁄₃ **cup** (75 mL) **fresh mint**

¹⁄₃ **cup** (75 mL) **fresh cilantro**

3 Tbsp. (45 mL) **peeled, chopped ginger**

2-3 garlic cloves

1¹⁄₂ Tbsp. (25 mL) **soy sauce**

1¹⁄₂ Tbsp. (25 mL) **fish sauce**

1¹⁄₂ Tbsp. (25 mL) **vegetable oil**

1¹⁄₂ Tbsp. (25 mL) **brown sugar**

1 Anaheim pepper, chopped

6 skinless, boneless chicken breast halves 2 lbs. (1 kg)

Process marinade ingredients in food processor or blender until finely chopped.

Arrange chicken in glass baking dish. Pour marinade over. Cover and refrigerate several hours or overnight. Remove chicken from marinade and grill until chicken is no longer pink in the middle.

Serve with Thai Noodle Salad on page 41.

LACE COOKIES

1 cup (250 mL) **sugar**

3 Tbsp. (45 mL) **flour**

1/4 tsp. (1 mL) **baking powder**

1/2 tsp. (2 mL) **salt**

1 egg

1 cup (250 mL) **rolled oats**

1/2 cup (125 mL)
butter, melted

1/2 tsp. (2 mL) **vanilla**

Mix sugar, flour, baking powder and salt in small bowl.

In medium bowl, beat egg. Add rolled oats, melted butter and vanilla. Blend together. Add sugar mixture to egg mixture and stir.

Preheat oven to 350°F (180°C). Line cookie sheets with foil, shiny side up. Drop only 6 tsps. of batter, 1 tsp. (5 mL) per cookie, onto each sheet. They spread out during baking and are very thin and lacy. Bake for 8-10 minutes. Watch carefully! They are cooked when they turn golden brown. Cool for 5 minutes. Peel off foil and snitch one!

A delicate cookie. Perfect with Sorbet on page 60 or Panna Cotta on page 58. Makes 3 dozen.

BERRY-TOPPED CHOCOLATE TORTE

²/₃ **cup** (150 mL) **ground almonds**

3 Tbsp. (45 mL) **flour**

pinch of salt

³/₄ **cup** (175 mL) **butter**

¹/₃ **cup** (75 mL) **cocoa powder**

¹/₂ **cup** (125 mL) **sugar**

3 eggs, separated

¹/₂ **cup** (125 mL) **sugar**

3 Tbsp. (45 mL) **Grand Marnier liqueur or orange juice**

1 cup (250 mL) **whipping cream**

1 Tbsp. (15 mL) **Grand Marnier liqueur**

2 cups (500 mL) **raspberries**

chocolate curls

Grease a 9" (23 cm) springform pan and line with parchment paper. In small bowl, combine almonds, flour and salt. Set aside.

Melt butter in saucepan and stir in cocoa and sugar.

In large bowl, beat egg yolks until thick; gradually blend in cocoa mixture. Stir in almond mixture.

In separate bowl, beat egg whites until stiff. Gradually add sugar. Fold whites into chocolate mixture. Pour into prepared pan and bake at 375°F (190°C) for 25 to 30 minutes, until toothpick comes out clean. Let cool in pan for 10 minutes. Run a knife around edge of torte and remove sides of springform pan.

Torte will fall in middle. (Don't worry, you can fill it with whipped cream!)

Drizzle 3 Tbsp. (45 mL) Grand Marnier over cake. Cool completely and wrap with plastic wrap. This can be stored in refrigerator for two days.

Whip cream and fold in Grand Marnier. Spread on torte and decorate with berries and chocolate curls. (See chef's tip.)

Serves 8.

VANILLA PANNA COTTA

1 Tbsp. (15 mL) **gelatin**

½ cup (125 mL) **milk**

3 cups (750 mL) **whipping cream**

½ cup (125 mL) **milk**

½ cup (125 mL) **sugar**

1 tsp. (5 mL) **vanilla**

Garnish:

mango

pineapple

raspberries

kiwi fruit

peaches

In large bowl, add gelatin to cold milk and let soften.

In saucepan, combine whipping cream, milk, sugar and vanilla and bring to a boil. Pour over gelatin mixture and stir until completely dissolved. Set bowl over very cold water and chill ½ hour, stirring occasionally, until almost set. Pour mixture into 8 individual ½ cup (125 mL) ramekins and store in refrigerator. Cover with plastic wrap if making the night before.

To serve, quickly dip ramekins in warm water to loosen sides. Invert onto individual serving plates and shake to release. Cut fruit into small pieces and arrange on each plate around panna cotta.

You'll never make anything else that's this good and this easy!
The texture is like velvet!
Serves 8.

*Use fully ripened
fruit to get the best flavour.*

PINEAPPLE, RHUBARB, WATERMELON AND MANGO SORBETS

Simple Syrup:

1½ cups (375 mL) **water**

1½ cups (375 mL)
berry sugar

Pineapple Sorbet:

**1 large whole pineapple,
peeled and cored**

2 cups (500 mL) **simple syrup**

2 Tbsp. (30 mL) **freshly
squeezed lemon juice**

Rhubarb Sorbet:

5 cups (1.25 L) **diced rhubarb**

1¼ cups (310 mL)
simple syrup

2 Tbsp. (30 mL) **freshly
squeezed lemon juice**

Watermelon Sorbet:

**¼ medium-sized
watermelon, skin and
seeds removed**

1 cup (250 mL) **simple syrup**

3 Tbsp. (45 mL) **freshly
squeezed lemon juice**

Mango Sorbet:

3 ripe mangoes, peeled

½ cup (125 mL) **simple syrup**

2 Tbsp. (30 mL) **freshly
squeezed lemon juice**

In small saucepan bring water and sugar to a boil. Simmer until sugar has dissolved. Yields 2½ cups (625 mL).

Cut pineapple into chunks and purée in food processor. Mix 2½ cups (625 mL) puréed pulp with simple syrup and lemon juice. Strain through sieve. Freeze in a 9x13" (23x33 cm) glass baking dish or an ice cream maker. When solid, break into pieces and pulse in chilled food processor until smooth. Store in plastic container in freezer for up to 2 weeks.

Purée rhubarb in food processor. Strain through sieve or cheesecloth, pressing to extract all of the juice. Discard pulp. Mix juice together with simple syrup and lemon juice and freeze in a 9x13" (23x33 cm) glass baking dish or an ice cream maker. When solid, break into pieces and pulse in chilled food processor until smooth. Store in plastic container in freezer for up to 2 weeks.

Cut watermelon in pieces and purée in food processor. Mix 3 cups (750 mL) of purée with simple syrup and lemon juice. Freeze in a 9x13" (23x33 cm) glass baking dish or an ice cream maker. When solid, break into pieces and pulse in chilled food processor until smooth. Store in plastic container in freezer for up to 2 weeks.

Cut mango pulp from pit and purée in food processor. Mix 1¾ cups (425 mL) mango purée with simple syrup and lemon juice. Strain through sieve. Freeze in a 9x13" (23x33 cm) glass baking dish or an ice cream maker. When solid, break into pieces. Pulse small batches at a time in a chilled food processor until smooth. Store in plastic container in freezer for up to 2 weeks.

Sorbet is so simple to make. Be sure to serve a combination of these refreshing flavours to your summer guests.

AUTUMN

Crunching leaves underfoot into a mottled palette of russets and golds. An earthy tang of woodsmoke carried on refreshingly crisp air. Geese and ducks form distant arrows in the sky, pointing south.

APPLES, CHEESE AND PORT

¹/₂ **lb.** (250 g)
**Imperial cheese
(cold-pack Cheddar),
crumbled**

¹/₂ **cup** (125 mL) **sour cream**

¹/₄ **cup** (60 mL) **port**

3-4 Granny Smith apples

fresh lemon juice

Using food processor or electric beater, blend cheese, sour cream and port until smooth.

Core apples and cut into wedges. Sprinkle with lemon juice.

Place cheese mixture in bowl and serve with apple wedges for dipping.

This may be made up to three days in advance and refrigerated. Cut apples just before serving.

Serve as an appetizer or after dinner.
Serves 6-8.

PEPPER QUESADILLAS WITH MANGO SALSA

6 oz. (170 g) **Monterey Jack cheese, grated**

4 x 6″ (4 x 15 cm) **flour tortillas**

1 red pepper, seeded, thinly sliced

1 yellow pepper, seeded, thinly sliced

1 jalapeño pepper, seeded and diced

¹/₂ red onion, thinly sliced

3 oz. (85 g) **chèvre (goat cheese) or feta cheese**

Mango Salsa:

1 mango

1 jalapeño pepper

¹/₂ cup (125 mL) **diced English cucumber**

2 Tbsp. (30 mL) **fresh lime juice**

2 Tbsp. (30 mL) **olive oil**

1 Tbsp. (15 mL) **chopped cilantro**

sour cream

Sprinkle ¹/₄ of the Monterey Jack on half of each tortilla.

———

Place 5-6 strips of red and yellow pepper on top of cheese, sprinkling ¹/₄ of jalapeño pepper over top. Top with a few strips of onion.

———

Crumble ¹/₄ of chèvre over top of mixture on each tortilla.
Fold each tortilla in half, pressing down lightly to seal. Set aside.

———

In medium non-stick frying pan over medium heat, cook one tortilla at a time for 1-2 minutes each side, until cheese has melted.

———

To make salsa, peel and dice mango. Seed and finely chop jalapeño. Peel, seed and finely dice cucumber. Mix mango, jalapeño and cucumber with lime juice and oil. Add cilantro.

———

To serve, cut each tortilla into 4 pieces. Pass the sour cream and salsa.

———

Always a hit!
Serves 4.

SPINACH, BACON AND GRUYÈRE SOUFFLÉ

4 slices bacon, cut into ¹/₂″ (1.5 cm) pieces

¹/₃ cup (75 mL) freshly grated Parmesan cheese

2 Tbsp. (30 mL) butter

1 medium onion, diced

6 Tbsp. (90 mL) flour

2 cups (500 mL) milk

5 egg yolks, room temperature (reserve whites)

salt and freshly ground pepper to taste

6 egg whites

1¹/₂ cups (375 mL) shredded, lightly packed Gruyère cheese

2 cups (500 mL) baby spinach leaves, lightly packed

Cook bacon until crisp. Drain on paper towel. Preheat oven to 400°F (200°C).

———

Butter a 2-quart (2 L) soufflé dish (must have straight sides). Dust sides and bottom with half of Parmesan.

———

In large saucepan, melt butter and sauté onions until soft (not browned), about 10 minutes. Add flour and cook, stirring constantly, for 2 minutes.

———

Pour milk slowly into onion mixture, stirring as you pour. Heat to just below boiling point, reduce to medium-low and cook, stirring constantly, until thick and smooth. Transfer to large bowl. Stir in bacon.

———

Whisk yolks into sauce one at a time. Season with salt and pepper and set aside. Cool completely.

———

In large bowl, beat egg whites until stiff peaks form. Fold half the whites into cooled sauce.

———

Wondering what to do with the extra egg yolk? Try making Almond Plum Tart on page 90.

———

Fold in Gruyère, remaining egg whites and spinach until egg white drifts disappear. **Do not overmix.** Pour into prepared soufflé dish and sprinkle remaining Parmesan evenly over top. Bake for 35-40 minutes. Serve immediately.

———

Perfect for brunch or dinner.
Serves 4.

ROASTED TOMATO BASIL SOUP

3 lbs. (1.5 kg) **ripe Roma tomatoes, cut in half lengthwise**

¼ cup (60 mL) **olive oil**

1 Tbsp. (15 mL) **salt**

1½ tsp. (7 mL) **ground pepper**

2 Tbsp. (30 mL) **olive oil**

2 cups (500 mL) **chopped onions**

6 garlic cloves, minced

¼ tsp. (1 mL) **red pepper flakes**

28 oz. (796 mL) **can plum tomatoes and juice**

2 cups (500 mL) **torn fresh basil leaves**

1 tsp. (5 mL) **thyme**

4 cups (1 L) **chicken stock**

Preheat oven to 400°F (200°C). Toss tomatoes with oil, salt and pepper. Spread in one layer on baking sheet and roast for 45 minutes.

In large pot over medium heat, heat oil and sauté onions, garlic and red pepper flakes until onions start to brown.

Add canned tomatoes, basil, thyme and chicken stock. Add oven-roasted tomatoes, including any liquid on baking sheet. Bring to a boil and simmer, uncovered, for 40 minutes. Purée in batches to a coarse mixture. Serve hot or cold.

Serves 6-8.

CHICKEN STOCK

Brown Chicken Stock:

3 lbs. (1.5 kg) **chicken bones (carcass or cooked bones and necks)**

1 cup (250 mL) **water**

2 Tbsp. (30 mL) **butter**

2 onions, coarsely chopped

3 carrots, peeled and coarsely chopped

3 stalks celery, coarsely chopped

12 cups (3 L) **water**

4 garlic cloves, peeled

4 bay leaves

Roast bones at 325°F (160°C) until golden brown, at least 1 hour. Remove bones to stockpot. Add water to roasting pan; scrape brown bits from bottom of roaster and add to stockpot.

————

While roasting bones, melt butter in large heavy-bottomed stockpot and sauté vegetables.

————

Add water, garlic and bay leaves to stockpot with bones and veggies and bring to boil. Reduce heat to simmer. Cook, covered, for at least 3½ hours. Strain stock, cool and skim off congealed fat.

————

For light chicken stock, follow the brown chicken stock recipe, but don't roast the bones.

————

Yields 11 cups of stock. Freeze in 1-cup (250 mL) containers.

————

We've always said we'd never have enough time (or the inclination) to make our own chicken stock – but Chef has convinced us otherwise! Choose an "at-home" day and get out the stockpot. The result is worth it!

Jicama (Hic-ama) is a root
vegetable from Central America.
It looks like a turnip with brown skin;
the texture of the white flesh is not
unlike a potato or apple. Peel it and
eat it raw drizzled with citrus juice,
or add it to your salad.

JICAMA AND CARROT COLESLAW

1/2 cup (125 mL)
pineapple juice

2 Tbsp. (30 mL) **freshly
squeezed lime juice**

2 Tbsp. (30 mL) **olive oil**

1/4 tsp. (1 mL) **ground
coriander or cumin**

**salt and freshly
ground pepper to taste**

1 lb. (500 g) **jicama**

3 large carrots

In large bowl, whisk together pineapple juice, lime juice, olive oil, coriander, salt and pepper. Set aside.

Cut off outer skin of the jicama and peel carrots. Slice vegetables into 3" (7.5 cm) long matchstick pieces. Whisk dressing again and gently toss with vegetables. Chill until ready to serve.

Consider this for your next potluck dinner.
Serves 6.

CHEF'S TIP

Rinsing the cooked spätzle in cold water will remove some of the starch and prevent the spätzle from sticking together.

SPÄTZLE

1½ **cups** (375 mL) **flour**

¼ **tsp.** (1 mL) **salt**

dash nutmeg, optional

———————

2 eggs, slightly beaten

½-¾ **cup** (125-175 mL) **milk**

———————

salt

8 cups (2 L) **water**

———————

¼ **cup** (60 mL) **butter**

1 small onion, chopped

salt and freshly ground pepper

———————

Mix together flour, salt and nutmeg.

———————

Add eggs and milk to flour mixture and stir to make a medium-thick batter.

———————

Add salt to water and bring to boil. Push batter through a spätzle maker and drop into boiling water. Simmer until tender, about 4-5 minutes, and drain.

———————

Melt butter in frying pan. Lightly sauté cooked spätzle with onion and seasonings, until golden.

———————

A Bavarian staple! Serve with Rib-Eye Steaks on page 50 and a jug of beer! Serves 6.

A spätzle maker is a must – inexpensive and amazing!

MUSHROOM TORTELLINI

4 slices bacon, chopped

2 Tbsp. (30 mL) **olive oil**

1 onion, sliced

2 cups (500 mL) **sliced mushrooms, stems removed**

1 garlic clove, minced

2 cups (500 mL) **whipping cream**

1 cup (250 mL) **chicken stock**

¼ **cup** (60 mL) **grated Parmesan cheese**

2 x 12 oz. (2 x 340 g) **pkgs. meat tortellini**

2 Tbsp. (30 mL) **chopped fresh parsley**

freshly ground pepper

Fry bacon and pour off fat.

Add oil to bacon in pan and heat. Lightly sauté onion, mushrooms and garlic.

Add cream and stock to vegetables and simmer for 15 minutes. Add Parmesan.

Cook tortellini according to package directions. Drain and add to sauce. Sprinkle with parsley and pepper.

Serves 6.

CREAMY RAVIOLI WITH SPINACH

1 garlic clove, minced

2 tsp. (10 mL) **olive oil**

1/2 cup (125 mL) **chicken stock**

2 cups (500 mL) **light cream**

1/4 cup (60 mL) **freshly grated Parmesan cheese**

1 lb. (500 g) **ricotta spinach ravioli**

2 cups (500 mL) **chopped fresh spinach**

8 oz. (250 g) **crab (optional)**

2 Tbsp. (30 mL) **chopped fresh dill**

2 fresh tomatoes

1/4 cup (60 mL) **freshly grated Parmesan cheese**

Over medium heat, sauté garlic in oil, add stock and simmer until reduced by half. Add cream and Parmesan, stirring until cheese has melted.

————

Cook ravioli according to package directions.

————

Add ravioli, spinach, crab and dill to sauce and heat through.

————

Blanch tomatoes in boiling water for 1 minute, then plunge into cold water. Peel off skins with a sharp knife. Cut in half and use a small spoon to remove seeds.

————

Chop tomatoes and spoon on top of each serving of ravioli.

————

Sprinkle with Parmesan.

————

Serves 6.

SEARED SCALLOPS WITH ORZO RISOTTO

Orzo Risotto:

1²/₃ cups (400 mL) **orzo**

1 Tbsp. (15 mL) **olive oil**

1 cup (250 mL) **diced mushrooms**

¹/₃ cup (75 mL) **diced onion**

¹/₃ cup (75 mL) **diced sun-dried tomatoes**

¹/₃ cup (75 mL) **diced red pepper**

2 cups (500 mL) **chicken stock**

¹/₂ cup (125 mL) **freshly grated Parmesan cheese**

2 Tbsp. (30 mL) **chopped parsley**

¹/₂ cup (125 mL) **whipping cream**

Scallops:

2 Tbsp. (30 mL) **olive oil**

16 large (³/₄ **lb.** (340 g)) **Nova Scotia scallops (large shrimp are an excellent substitute)**

salt and freshly ground pepper to taste

freshly grated Parmesan cheese

Cook orzo according to package directions and set aside.

In large heavy pot, heat oil and sauté mushrooms, onion, sun-dried tomatoes and red pepper until soft.

Add stock and bring to a boil.

Stir in orzo, Parmesan and parsley. Add cream and simmer gently, stirring frequently, until mixture is creamy but not runny, about 20 minutes.

Heat oil in very hot pan. Season scallops with salt and pepper and sear until brown on outside but just opaque in the middle.

Sprinkle Parmesan over risotto and top with scallops.

Awesome with asparagus! An elegant dinner for 4.

CHEF'S TIP

*Make this a day ahead.
Not only will the flavours be mellow
...so will you!!!*

BRAISED SHORT RIBS

¹/₃ **cup** (75 mL) **flour**

salt and pepper to taste

¹/₂ **tsp.** (2 mL) **paprika**

3-4 lbs. (about 2 kg)
beef short ribs, bone in

2 Tbsp. (30 mL) **vegetable oil**

2 medium onions

¹/₂ **cup** (125 mL)
tomato sauce

¹/₂ **cup** (125 mL)
barbecue sauce

2 Tbsp. (30 mL) **molasses**

2 Tbsp. (30 mL) **cider vinegar**

Combine flour, salt, pepper and paprika. Trim excess fat from ribs.
Dredge ribs in flour mixture and brown in oil on all sides. Remove to casserole.

Chop onion into large chunks and place on top of browned ribs.

Whisk tomato sauce, barbecue sauce, molasses and cider vinegar together
in saucepan. Bring to a boil and pour over ribs and onions. Cover and bake
at 275°F (140°C) for 3-4 hours.

*On a cool fall night your family will delight in the taste of barbecue.
Serve with mashed potatoes and a green vegetable.
Serves 4.*

PAELLA

2 **Tbsp.** (30 mL) **olive oil**

4 **spicy sausages (chorizo or Italian)**

8 **chicken thighs**

———————

1/2 **red pepper, diced**

1/2 **green pepper, diced**

3 **garlic cloves, minced**

1 **onion, chopped**

———————

2 **large tomatoes, peeled and diced**

2 **tsp.** (10 mL) **paprika**

2 **pinches saffron**

———————

3 1/2 **cups** (875 mL) **chicken stock**

2 1/2 **cups** (625 mL) **Arborio rice (white short grain), uncooked**

1 **cup** (250 mL) **frozen peas**

———————

1/2 **lb.** (250 g) **fresh mussels, rinsed in cold water (shells tightly closed)**

1/2 **lb.** (250 g) **fresh clams, rinsed in cold water (shells tightly closed)**

1/2 **lb.** (250 g) **prawns, rinsed in cold water**

8 **crab claws**

salt and freshly ground pepper

———————

Heat oil in large frying pan. Fry sausage, remove from pan, cool and cut into slices. In same pan, brown chicken thighs. Add sausage.

———————

Add peppers, garlic and onion to mixture in frying pan. Gently sauté until vegetables are softened.

———————

Add tomatoes, paprika and saffron to mixture and blend thoroughly.

———————

Add chicken stock and rice to mixture, cover and bring to a boil. Simmer for 10-15 minutes. Stir in peas.

———————

Transfer mixture to large shallow casserole or paella pan. Arrange seafood on top. Cover and place in a 350°F (180°C) oven for approximately 20 minutes. Remove and let stand for about 10 minutes.

———————

Serve from baking dish and pass the salt and pepper grinder.

———————

Paella (pi-AY-yuh) – we can't pronounce it, but we can sure tell you how to make it! Any combination of fresh seafood works in this traditional Spanish favourite. Great for entertaining! Serve with a robust red wine and a large bowl for the shells! Serves 8-10.

HERB-ROASTED CHICKEN

4 lb. (2 kg) **roasting chicken**

salt and freshly ground pepper

————

1 Tbsp. (15 mL) **chopped fresh sage**

1 Tbsp. (15 mL) **chopped fresh thyme**

1/2 tsp. (2 mL) **chopped fresh oregano**

1/2 tsp. (2 mL) **chopped fresh rosemary**

salt and freshly ground pepper

————

4 thin lemon slices, seeds removed

————

2 Tbsp. (30 mL) **butter, melted**

————

Preheat oven to 350°F (180°C). Rinse chicken under cold water and pat dry. Season inside and out with salt and pepper.

————

In small bowl, mix together sage, thyme, oregano, rosemary, salt and pepper. Using your fingers, loosen skin of chicken over breast by sliding fingers carefully between skin and flesh. Slip herbs inside pocket on each breast half.

————

Tuck 2 lemon slices into each breast side pocket. Tie chicken legs together with kitchen string.

————

Brush melted butter over chicken.

————

Roast chicken for 20 minutes per pound, or until thermometer in thigh reads 180°F (83°C). Cover loosely with foil and let stand 10 minutes before carving.

————

Fresh herbs are a must for this recipe!

NO–FUSS MOROCCAN CHICKEN

1¹/₂ lbs. (750 g) **boneless, skinless chicken breast halves**

2 Tbsp. (30 mL) **vegetable oil**

¹/₂ cup (125 mL) **chopped onion**

1 garlic clove, minced

2 cups (500 mL) **salsa**

¹/₂ cup (125 mL) **water**

¹/₄ cup (60 mL) **currants**

2 Tbsp. (30 mL) **liquid honey**

1¹/₂ tsp. (7 mL) **cumin**

1 tsp. (5 mL) **cinnamon**

¹/₂ cup (125 mL) **toasted slivered almonds**

Preheat oven to 325°F (160°C). Brown chicken in oil and place in baking dish.

Lightly sauté onion and garlic. Spoon over chicken.

Combine salsa, water, currants, honey, cumin and cinnamon. Pour over chicken. Cover and bake for 1 hour.

Sprinkle with almonds.

Serve with rice or couscous.
Serves 4.

ROASTED PORK TENDERLOIN WITH CARAMELIZED APPLES AND MUSTARD SAUCE

3 pork tenderloins

1 tsp. (5 mL) **freshly ground pepper**

1/2 tsp. (2 mL) **salt**

1/2 tsp. (2 mL) **chopped fresh rosemary**

2 Tbsp. (30 mL) **olive oil**

Mustard Sauce:

1/2 cup (125 mL) **white wine**

1 Tbsp. (15 mL) **Dijon mustard**

Caramelized Apples:

1/4 cup (60 mL) **butter**

3 cups (750 mL) **sliced cooking apples**

1/2 cup (125 mL) **brown sugar**

Season pork on all sides with pepper, salt and rosemary. Heat oil in large skillet over high heat. Add pork tenderloins and sear on both sides until just brown, about 2 minutes per side. Place seared tenderloins in roasting pan and set aside. Preheat oven to 350°F (180°C).

To make Mustard Sauce, remove skillet from heat to cool slightly. Return skillet to medium heat and add white wine, scraping pan to loosen any meat bits. Cook 1-2 minutes until slightly reduced. Whisk in mustard, then remove skillet from heat; set aside.

Roast pork about 30 minutes or until meat thermometer registers 170°F (77°C).

To caramelize apples, melt butter in medium sauté pan. Add apples and sprinkle on brown sugar. Cook until liquid is syrupy but apples are still firm, 3 to 4 minutes.

Reheat Mustard Sauce, adding any juices from roasting pan. Add tenderloins to skillet and cook briefly, just enough to coat with sauce, about 1 minute per side.

To serve, slice pork tenderloins diagonally into 1/4" (1 cm) thick pieces. Arrange on individual plates and spoon warm Caramelized Apples on the side.

Excellent served with roasted new potatoes.
Serves 4-6.

VEGGIE STACKS

For one stack:

¹/₄″ (1 cm) **slice eggplant
or portobello mushroom**

¹/₄″ (1 cm) **slice red onion**

¹/₄″ (1 cm) **slice
bocconcini cheese**

¹/₄″ (1 cm) **slice
fresh tomato**

grated Asiago cheese

————

Assemble stacks by layering one slice of eggplant, red onion, bocconcini and tomato. Sprinkle with grated Asiago. If you prefer, replace eggplant with a slice of portobello mushroom. Place stacks on cookie sheet and bake at 375°F (190°C) for about 20 minutes, until cheese melts and veggies soften.

————

Great with roast beef or steak.
Allow one stack per person.

HERBED SPAGHETTI SQUASH

1 medium spaghetti squash

¼ cup (60 mL) **olive oil**

¼ cup (60 mL) **chopped
fresh chives**

1 Tbsp. (15 mL) **chopped
fresh parsley**

1 Tbsp. (15 mL) **chopped
fresh basil**

1 tsp. (5 mL) **chopped
fresh rosemary**

1 garlic clove, minced

1 tsp. (5 mL) **freshly
squeezed lemon juice**

**salt and freshly ground
pepper to taste**

¼ cup (60 mL) **freshly
grated Parmesan cheese**

Preheat oven to 350°F (180°C). Cut squash lengthwise and remove seeds and membranes. Place cut-side down in baking dish. Add small amount of water and bake for 40 minutes, or until fork tender.
OR
To microwave, place cut-side down in microwavable baking dish.
Add small amount of water, cover and cook 10 minutes, or until fork tender.
Set aside to cool.

In food processor, add oil, chives, parsley, basil, rosemary, garlic and lemon juice. Blend until thoroughly mixed and smooth.

Using fork, scrape cooled squash into bowl. Season with salt and pepper, add herb mixture and toss to coat. Place squash in shallow baking dish. Sprinkle with cheese and set aside. Warm in oven before serving.

Serves 4.

SMILE

*If I could lose 30 lbs. –
I'd be down to the weight I never
thought I'd be up to.*

CARROT SWEET POTATO PURÉE

1 lb. (500 g) **carrots**

1 large **sweet potato**

———

2 Tbsp. (30 mL) **cream**

1 Tbsp. (15 mL) **butter**

¼ tsp. (1 mL) **salt**

dash of **cayenne**

———

additional butter

———

Peel carrots and potato and chop into pieces. Cook in boiling salted water until tender. Drain. Transfer vegetables to food processor and blend until smooth.

———

Add cream, butter, salt and cayenne to purée. Process until well blended and butter melts. Transfer to ovenproof dish.

———

Dot with butter and bake at 350°F (180°C) for 15-20 minutes.

———

A sweet twist to mashed potatoes. Can be made ahead.
Serves 4-6.

ROASTED SWEET POTATO WEDGES

3 sweet potatoes

1 Tbsp. (15 mL) **olive oil**

---

1 Tbsp. (15 mL) **brown sugar**

1/2 tsp. (2 mL) **chili powder**

1/2 tsp. (2 mL) **salt**

1/8–1/4 tsp. (0.5-1 mL)
cayenne pepper

Preheat oven to 400°F (200°C). Peel potatoes and cut into 1" (2.5 cm) wedges.

———

In large bowl, toss potatoes with oil. Mix sugar and seasonings together. Sprinkle on potatoes and stir until evenly coated.

———

Spread on non-stick baking sheet large enough to hold potatoes without overcrowding.

———

Roast potatoes for 30 minutes, turning every 10 minutes until tender and browned.

———

Serve with ham or pork roast.
Serves 4.

OVEN-ROASTED AUTUMN VEGETABLES

1 large sweet potato, peeled and cut into 1" (2.5 cm) **cubes**

1 fennel bulb (1lb. (500 g)**), scrubbed, trimmed and cut into wedges**

6 small red potatoes, scrubbed and quartered

3-4 parsnips, peeled and chopped

4 large shallots, peeled and cut into quarters

2 Tbsp. (30 mL) **olive oil**

1 Tbsp. (15 mL) **balsamic vinegar**

1 tsp. (5 mL) **coarse salt**

1 Tbsp. (15 mL) **balsamic vinegar**

Preheat oven to 425°F (220°C). In large roasting pan toss sweet potato, fennel, red potatoes, parsnips, and shallots with oil and 1 Tbsp. (15 mL) vinegar and salt. Roast uncovered for 30-35 minutes, stirring and tossing once or twice, until vegetables are lightly browned and tender.

Place roasted vegetables in large serving bowl. Sprinkle with 1 Tbsp. (15 mL) vinegar.

Serves 4-6.

BETTER-THAN-MOM'S OATMEAL COOKIES

1 cup (250 mL) **butter or margarine**

1 cup (250 mL) **sugar**

1 cup (250 mL) **brown sugar**

---

2 large eggs

2 tsp. (10 mL) **vanilla**

1½ cups (375 mL) **flour**

1⅛ tsp. (5.5 mL) **baking soda**

1 tsp. (5 mL) **salt**

1 tsp. (5 mL) **cinnamon**

½ tsp. (2 mL) **mace**

½ tsp. (2 mL) **nutmeg**

½ tsp. (2 mL) **ground cloves**

---

3 cups (750 mL) **rolled oats**

1 cup (250 mL) **chopped walnuts or pecans**

1 cup (250 mL) **golden raisins**

In large bowl, cream butter and sugars until light and fluffy.

Beat in eggs and vanilla.

In medium-sized bowl, mix flour, soda, salt, cinnamon, mace, nutmeg and cloves together. Gradually add dry ingredients to creamed mixture, mixing until completely blended.

Mix in oats, nuts and raisins.

Preheat oven to 350°F (180°C). Lightly grease cookie sheets and drop teaspoonfuls of dough about 2" (5 cm) apart. Flatten each mound slightly. Bake for 8-10 minutes for a soft cookie, 12 minutes for a crunchy cookie. Cool on wire rack.

Talk about raves! Makes about 4 dozen cookies.

ALMOND PLUM TART

1¹/₄ cups (310 mL) **flour**

1 Tbsp. (15 mL) **icing sugar**

pinch of salt

¹/₂ cup (125 mL) **butter, cut into small pieces**

1 egg yolk

2 Tbsp. (30 mL) **ice water**

1¹/₂ cups (375 mL) **chopped almonds**

³/₄ cup (175 mL) **sugar**

¹/₄ cup (60 mL) **butter, room temperature**

2 Tbsp. (30 mL) **flour**

¹/₄ cup (60 mL) **amaretto liqueur**

2 eggs

1¹/₄ lbs. (625 g) **purple plums, pitted and thinly sliced (4-5 large plums)**

2 Tbsp. (30 mL) **butter, cut into bits**

2 Tbsp. (30 mL) **sugar**

2 Tbsp. (30 mL) **toasted slivered almonds**

In food processor, combine flour, sugar and salt. Process briefly to mix.

Add butter and process until mixture forms small pea-sized pieces.

With processor running, add egg yolk and gradually add ice water. Process until dough just begins to come together and will hold shape when pressed. Press into thick disk and roll out into a 12" (30 cm) round. Place over a 10" (25 cm) tart pan with removable bottom. Ease pastry over bottom and sides of the pan, pressing gently into place. Roll rolling pin over top of pan to trim excess pastry. Place tart pan on baking sheet and set aside.

In food processor, mix almonds, sugar, butter, flour and amaretto. Pulse until crumbly mixture forms.

Add eggs and process for 10 seconds. Spread mixture in even layer in pastry-lined pan.

Preheat oven to 400°F (200°C).

Arrange plum slices in overlapping circles on filling (be generous). Be sure to fit plum slices tightly together. Cover filling completely.

Dot plums with butter and dust with sugar. Bake 40-45 minutes, until tart has browned. Transfer to rack and let cool. Garnish with almonds.

Serve at room temperature.

Serve with Sauce Anglaise, page 133, or vanilla ice cream for the finishing touch. Serves 8-10.

POACHED PEARS IN RED WINE

8 Bosc pears

2 cups (500 mL) **red wine**

zest of one lemon

2 Tbsp. (30 mL)
fresh lemon juice

1 cup (250 mL) **sugar**

1 stick cinnamon

1 tsp. (5 mL) **vanilla**

Garnish:

soft whipped cream

chocolate curls

mint leaves

Peel pears with vegetable peeler, keeping stems intact. Trim bottoms so they can stand. Place in deep saucepan.

In another saucepan, pour in red wine, lemon zest, lemon juice, sugar, cinnamon and vanilla. Bring to a boil. Pour over pears and add enough boiling water to cover. Simmer very slowly, until just tender. Test by inserting a skewer. Remove pears carefully to a dish. Rapidly boil liquid and reduce until only one cup (250 mL) remains. Pour over pears and cool. (Can be refrigerated overnight.)

To serve, spoon some liquid onto individual dessert plates and place a pear on each plate. Garnish with dollop of whipped cream, chocolate curl and mint leaf.

Serves 8.

APPLE CRISP WITH TOFFEE SAUCE

½ cup (125 mL) **sugar**

¼ cup (60 mL) **flour**

1 Tbsp. (15 mL) **cinnamon**

½ tsp. (2 mL) **salt**

1 cup (250 mL) **light cream**

1 Tbsp. (15 mL) **freshly squeezed lemon juice**

8 **Granny Smith apples, peeled, cored and sliced in wedges**

1½ cups (375 mL) **flour**

1 cup (250 mL) **packed brown sugar**

2 tsp. (10 mL) **cinnamon**

¼ tsp. (1 mL) **salt**

¾ cup (175 mL) **cold butter**

Toffee Sauce:

1 cup (250 mL) **packed brown sugar**

½ cup (125 mL) **butter**

½ cup (125 mL) **light cream**

Preheat oven to 350°F (180°C). Butter 9x13" (23x33 cm) baking dish.
In large bowl, mix together sugar, flour, cinnamon and salt. Gradually add cream and lemon juice, stirring until combined.

————

Toss apples in cream mixture. Spoon into prepared pan.

————

Mix together flour, brown sugar, cinnamon and salt. Cut in butter with pastry blender until mixture is crumbly. Spread over apples and pat down lightly. Bake for 45 minutes.

————

To prepare Toffee Sauce, combine sauce ingredients in saucepan and stir over low heat until sugar is dissolved. Simmer until sauce thickens.

————

Serve warm with Toffee Sauce. An excellent dessert for large family gatherings – down home and delicious! Serves 10-12.

OATMEAL CRISPIES

1 cup (250 mL)
butter, softened

¹/₂ cup (125 mL) **sugar**

1 cup (250 mL) **flour**

1¹/₂ cups (375 mL)
rolled oats

icing sugar

Preheat oven to 350°F (180°C).

In large bowl, beat butter and sugar together until creamy.

Combine flour and rolled oats. Mix into creamed mixture. Shape dough into medium-sized balls and place about 3" (7.5 cm) apart on cookie sheets. Flatten with fork dipped in water. Bake for 10 minutes. Cool before removing from cookie sheets.

When completely cool, generously dust with icing (confectioner's) sugar.

You MUST try these – they're very more-ish!
Makes 3 dozen cookies.

WINTER

A time of brief days and brilliant sunshine…where the snow has its own language of squeaks and whispers… where cheeks redden in the bracing air… and bare branches fracture the sky…

BRANDIED BLUE CHEESE, WALNUT AND PEAR CROSTINI

4 oz. (125 g) **blue cheese, crumbled**

2 Tbsp. (30 mL) **butter**

----

2 Tbsp. (30 mL) **brandy**

¼ cup (60 mL) **coarsely chopped walnuts**

----

16 x ½" (16 x 1.5 cm) **baguette slices**

1 ripe pear, thinly sliced

Bring cheese and butter to room temperature (30 minutes). Mash with fork until smooth.

Stir brandy and walnuts into cheese mixture.

Place baguette slices on cookie sheet. Toast one side under broiler. Turn and place slice of pear on untoasted side. Top pear with teaspoonful of cheese mixture.

Broil 4-5" (10-13 cm) from heat for about 2 minutes, or until cheese melts and is bubbly.

Serves 8.

CRAB CAKES
WITH ROASTED RED PEPPER AÏOLI

Béchamel Sauce:

2 Tbsp. (30 mL) **butter**

2 Tbsp. (30 mL) **flour**

1 cup (250 mL) **hot milk**

1 bay leaf

1 lb. (500 g) **crabmeat
or mock crab**

½ red pepper, finely diced

2 green onions, diced

½ cup (125 mL)
fresh breadcrumbs

½ tsp. (2 mL) **cayenne**

1½ tsp. (7 mL) **lemon juice**

dash Worcestershire sauce

salt and pepper to taste

---

1 cup (250 mL) **breadcrumbs**

¼ cup (60 mL) **butter**

Roasted Red Pepper Aïoli:

½ cup (125 mL)
**roasted red peppers
(found in your deli section)**

½ cup (125 mL) **mayonnaise**

1 garlic clove, minced

1 tsp. (5 mL) **lemon juice**

Melt butter in medium-sized saucepan and add flour. Mix thoroughly and cook over medium heat for about 3 minutes. Do not brown.

Gradually stir hot milk into flour mixture until it forms a smooth sauce. Add bay leaf and cook for just a few minutes. Chill. Remove bay leaf from sauce.

Squeeze any liquid from crabmeat and add crab to Béchamel Sauce. If using mock crab, chop in food processor. (Don't let the chef catch you using mock crab!)

Add red pepper, onion, breadcrumbs, cayenne, lemon juice, Worcestershire sauce, salt and pepper to sauce. Mix thoroughly. Cover and chill for 30 minutes or overnight.

Form crab mixture into 2" (5 cm) balls for appetizer-sized cakes (larger for main course). Roll in breadcrumbs and flatten. Melt butter and brown each side.

To make aïoli, purée red peppers. Add mayonnaise, garlic and lemon juice to roasted red pepper purée.

Refrigerate until serving.

These can be made one day ahead and cooked just before serving.
Serve warm with Roasted Red Pepper Aïoli.
Makes 36 appetizers.

CITRUS CREAM PULL-APARTS

1 lb. (500 g) **frozen dinner roll dough**

OR

1 lb. (500 g) **loaf frozen bread dough**

½ **cup** (125 mL) **dried cranberries**

½ **cup** (125 mL) **dried apricots, chopped**

2 Tbsp. (30 mL) **butter, melted**

½ **cup** (125 mL) **sugar**

½ **cup** (125 mL) **cream cheese, softened**

1 Tbsp. (15 mL) **grated lemon zest**

1 Tbsp. (15 mL) **grated orange zest**

2 Tbsp. (30 mL) **orange juice**

2 Tbsp. (30 mL) **fresh lemon juice**

1 cup (250 mL) **icing (confectioner's) sugar**

Thaw dinner roll dough at room temperature for 30 minutes. Cut rolls in half.
OR
Thaw frozen bread dough at room temperature for 30 minutes. Cut loaf in half and cut each half into 12 pieces.

———

Place half the rolls in greased 2-quart (2 L) bundt pan. Sprinkle rolls with half the cranberries and apricots. Add remaining rolls.

———

Brush rolls with butter and sprinkle on remaining cranberries and apricots. Cover with clean tea towel and let rise for 30 minutes.

———

Cream sugar and cheese together.

———

Add lemon zest, orange zest and juice to creamed mixture and beat until smooth. Pour over rolls. Cover with plastic wrap and leave on counter overnight.

———

In the morning, preheat oven to 350°F (180°C) and bake rolls for 40 minutes, checking the last 10 minutes. Cover loosely with foil if buns become too brown. Cool 15 minutes. Place plate over pan and invert.

———

Combine juice and sugar. Drizzle over rolls. Just pull apart to serve.

———

*Overnight wonder! Brunch Bonanza!
Serves 8-10.*

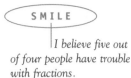
HAM, FONTINA AND SPINACH STRATA

1 large baguette

1/4 cup (60 mL) **butter, melted**

2 Tbsp. (30 mL) **olive oil**

2 medium onions, chopped

1 lb. (500 g) **piece of ham, cut into 1/2"** (1.5 cm) **cubes**

4 large eggs

4 cups (1 L) **milk**

1 tsp. (5 mL) **salt**

1/4 tsp. (1 mL) **grated nutmeg**

pepper to taste

6 cups (1.5 L) **(about 2 med. bunches) fresh spinach, coarsely chopped**

3/4 lb. (375 g) **Fontina or Gruyère cheese, grated**

Preheat broiler. Cut baguette diagonally into 3/4" (2 cm) thick slices. Brush both sides with butter and toast on baking sheet 3" (7.5 cm) from heat until golden, about 30 seconds each side.

Heat oil in large frying pan over medium-high heat. Add onions and stir until golden. Add ham and sauté until lightly browned. Set aside.

In large bowl whisk together eggs, milk, salt, nutmeg and pepper. Add toasted bread and toss gently. Transfer saturated bread to shallow 3-quart (3 L) casserole, slightly overlapping slices. Place spinach and ham mixture between slices. Pour remaining egg mixture over all.

Sprinkle Fontina over strata, lifting slices with spatula to allow cheese to fall between all slices. Preheat oven to 350°F (180°C). Bake strata in middle of oven for 45 minutes to 1 hour, or until puffed and edges of bread are golden and custard is set.

This can be assembled a day ahead. Cover and refrigerate.

A versatile dish for brunch or dinner.
Serves 6-8.

PEAR AND STILTON SALAD

Dressing:

¹/₄ **cup** (60 mL) **fresh lemon juice**

¹/₄ **cup** (60 mL) **canola oil**

1 **Tbsp.** (15 mL) **liquid honey**

2 **tsp.** (10 mL) **grainy mustard or Dijon mustard**

butter lettuce

2 **fresh, ripe pears, cored and sliced**

4 **oz.** (125 g) **Stilton cheese, crumbled, or Asiago cheese, shaved**

¹/₄ **cup** (60 mL) **fresh pine nuts, toasted**

In small bowl, whisk together lemon juice, oil, honey and mustard.

————

Place lettuce leaves on individual plates. Arrange sliced pears on top and sprinkle with Stilton and pine nuts.

————

Drizzle dressing over top.

————

Shop ahead for this salad so you can ripen the pears! A delicious starter salad for 4.

POMEGRANATE AND FETA SALAD

1 head romaine lettuce, washed and torn

1 bunch spinach, stems removed, washed and torn

seeds of 1 pomegranate

1/4 cup (60 mL) **toasted pine nuts**

1/2 cup (125 mL) **crumbled feta cheese**

Dressing:

1/3 cup (75 mL) **olive oil**

1 Tbsp. (15 mL) **red wine vinegar**

2 Tbsp. (30 mL) **maple syrup**

1 tsp. (5 mL) **Dijon mustard**

1/2 tsp. (2 mL) **oregano**

salt and freshly ground pepper

Toss lettuce and spinach together in large salad bowl.

Add pomegranate seeds, pine nuts and feta.

Whisk dressing ingredients together and store in refrigerator. Toss with salad ingredients just before serving.

The pomegranate seeds add sparkle to this salad!
Serves 6.

ROASTED VEGETABLE MANICOTTI WITH CHEESE SAUCE

1 onion

2 cups (500 mL) **chopped broccoli**

2 cups (500 mL) **chopped cauliflower**

2 cups (500 mL) **chopped carrot**

1 red pepper

3 Tbsp. (45 mL) **olive oil**

1 Tbsp. (15 mL) **balsamic vinegar**

2 garlic cloves, minced

3 cups (750 mL) **spinach**

1 cup (250 mL) **freshly grated Parmesan cheese**

1 cup (250 mL) **ricotta cheese**

1 egg, beaten

2 slices bread

1/2 cup (125 mL) **fresh parsley**

1/2 cup (125 mL) **fresh basil**

salt and pepper to taste

16 manicotti shells

2 x 14 oz. (2 x 398 mL) **cans tomato sauce**

Asiago cheese, grated

Chop vegetables into 1" (2.5 cm) pieces. Toss with oil, vinegar and garlic. Roast at 350°F (180°C) for 40 minutes, stirring occasionally.

———

Mix spinach with hot vegetables and set aside to cool. Pulse vegetables in food processor to a coarse texture.

———

Mix together Parmesan, ricotta and egg. Blend with vegetables.

———

In food processor, whirl bread, herbs and seasonings. Add to vegetable mixture.

———

Cook manicotti according to package directions. Drain well. Fill with vegetable mixture using spoon or very small knife. Pour tomato sauce in bottom of two 9x13" (22x33 cm) baking dishes and arrange stuffed manicotti in each baking dish. Make cheese sauce on page 111 and pour over manicotti. Sprinkle with grated Asiago. Bake at 350°F (180°C) for about 30 minutes.

———

Serves 8-10.

CHEESE SAUCE

3 Tbsp. (45 mL) **butter**

3 Tbsp. (45 mL) **flour**

3 cups (750 mL) **milk**

2 cups (500 mL) **grated mozzarella or Swiss cheese**

1 tsp. (5 mL) **Worcestershire sauce**

dash hot pepper sauce

salt and pepper to taste

Melt butter over medium heat and blend in flour. Cook for 1 minute, stirring constantly until smooth and bubbly. Reduce heat to medium-low.

Gradually add milk, stirring constantly until thickened.

Add cheese, Worcestershire and hot pepper sauce to thickened mixture and stir until cheese is melted. Add salt and pepper.

SMILE

I've always wanted to
be somebody, but I should have
been more specific.

FOREST MUSHROOM CHOWDER

2 Tbsp. (30 mL) **vegetable oil**

1 garlic clove, minced

¹/₂ cup (125 mL) **sliced onions**

¹/₂ cup (125 mL) **diced carrots**

3 cups (750 mL) **sliced
wild mushrooms (chanterelle,
morel, shiitake, oyster)**

—————

3 cups (750 mL) **chicken stock**

2 cups (500 mL)
whipping cream

—————

¹/₄ cup (60 mL)
diced potatoes

¹/₄ cup (60 mL) **frozen
corn niblets**

¹/₂ apple, peeled and diced

2 bay leaves

3 Tbsp. (45 mL) **sherry**

2 Tbsp. (30 mL)
chopped parsley

**salt and freshly
ground pepper**

—————

In large saucepan or Dutch oven, heat oil and sauté garlic, onions, carrots and mushrooms. Do not brown.

—————

Add stock and cream to vegetable mixture. Bring to a boil and reduce heat to simmer.

—————

Add potatoes, corn niblets, apple, bay leaves, sherry and parsley to soup. Simmer about ¹/₂ hour. Remove bay leaves and season with salt and pepper.

—————

A soup made with care is a delight to the soul. (So there!)
Serves 6.

ROASTED SQUASH SOUP
WITH APPLE AND BRIE

1 large butternut squash

1 carrot

1 medium onion

1 leek, white portion only

2 Tbsp. (30 mL) **butter**

8 cups (2 L) **chicken stock**

1 apple, peeled and chopped

1 bay leaf

1 tsp. (5 mL) **sugar**

**salt and freshly
ground pepper**

8 oz. (250 g) **Brie cheese**

snipped chives

Cut squash in half lengthwise and remove seeds. Place cut-side down on pan and bake at 350°F (180°C) until tender, about 45 minutes (or microwave cut-side down in a small amount of water, covered, about 10 minutes).

Chop carrot, onion and leek into 1" (2.5 cm) pieces and place in large pot. Gently sauté in butter. Do not brown. Scrape flesh from cooked squash and add to vegetables. Add stock and bring to a boil.

Add apple, bay leaf and sugar to stock mixture. Simmer, uncovered, for 40 minutes. Remove bay leaf and purée soup in batches. Season with salt and pepper to taste.

Slice off outer skin of Brie and cut into $^{1}/_{2}$" (1.5 cm) pieces. Place cheese in bottom of soup bowls and fill with hot soup. Garnish with chives.

Serves 6-8.

HUNTER'S WILD RICE

3½ cups (825 mL) **chicken stock**

¼ cup (60 mL) **sherry**

2 Tbsp. (30 mL) **soy sauce**

1 tsp. (5 mL) **chili sauce**

1 Tbsp. (15 mL) **grated orange zest**

salt to taste

3 Tbsp. (45 mL) **butter**

½ cup (125 mL) **minced onion**

3 garlic cloves, minced

1½ cups rice (375 mL) **(wild/brown mix)**

⅔ cup (150 mL) **currants**

½ cup (125 mL) **chopped fresh cilantro or fresh parsley**

¾ cup (175 mL) **toasted pecan halves**

Combine stock, sherry, soy sauce, chili sauce, orange zest and salt in medium bowl; set-aside.

————

Melt butter in saucepan and sauté onion and garlic. Add rice and sauté a few minutes.

————

Add currants and stock mixture to rice. Cover and bring to a boil. Lower heat and simmer until rice is tender, about 30-45 minutes, or until liquid is absorbed.

————

Stir in cilantro and pecans just before serving.

————

Ideal with fowl and game.
Serves 6-8.

CHEF'S TIP

To toast almonds, place on cookie sheet in a 350°F (180°C) oven for about 5 minutes. Watch closely!

CHICKEN, ARTICHOKE AND WILD RICE CASSEROLE

3 cups (750 mL) **water**

1 cup (250 mL) **wild rice**

1/2 tsp. (2 mL) **salt**

1 Tbsp. (15 mL) **butter**

1 cup (250 mL) **chopped onion**

1 cup (250 mL) **thinly sliced celery**

1 cup (250 mL) **shredded carrot**

1 3/4 cups (425 mL) **chicken stock**

2 cups (500 mL) **light cream**

1/4 cup (60 mL) **flour**

3/4 tsp. (3 mL) **salt**

2 Tbsp. (30 mL) **sherry**

freshly ground pepper

3 cups (750 mL) **cooked cubed chicken**

14 oz. (398 g) **can artichokes, drained and chopped**

1/3 cup (75 mL) **toasted sliced almonds**

In medium-sized saucepan, bring water to a boil. Stir in rice and salt. Cover and simmer 45-55 minutes, or until rice is tender but still chewy. Drain rice in colander.

___

Melt butter in large frying pan over medium heat. Add onion, celery and carrot; cook 10 minutes, stirring occasionally, until softened.

___

Add stock to veggies in frying pan and bring to a boil.

___

In bowl, whisk cream and flour until smooth. Gradually whisk into boiling broth. Add salt, sherry and pepper. Bring to a boil. Reduce heat and simmer 5 minutes, stirring occasionally. Add rice to sauce.

___

Add chicken and artichokes to sauce and mix well. Pour mixture into shallow 2 1/2-3-quart (2-3 L) baking dish. Cover and bake at 350°F (180°C) for 35-40 minutes, or until hot and bubbly.

___

Sprinkle with almonds.

___

Serve with Avocado and Grapefruit Salad on page 13.
Serves 8-10.

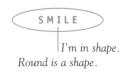

SMILE

I'm in shape.
Round is a shape.

SPAGHETTI BASIL TORTE

1 lb. (500 g) **spaghetti**

¹/₂ cup (125 mL) **grated Parmesan cheese**

1¹/₂ cups (375 mL) **ricotta cheese**

2 tsp. (10 mL) **Italian seasoning**

2 eggs, beaten

¹/₂ cup (125 mL) **chopped fresh basil or 2 Tbsp.** (30 mL) **dried**

4-5 medium tomatoes, sliced

8 oz. (250 g) **grated provolone cheese**

salt and freshly grated pepper to taste

Heat oven to 350°F (180°C). Spray a 9" (23 cm) springform pan with cooking spray. In large pot, cook spaghetti as directed on package. Rinse with cold water and drain.

Toss Parmesan, ricotta, Italian seasoning and eggs with spaghetti until well coated.

Press half the spaghetti mixture in bottom of pan. Sprinkle with half the basil. Layer with half the tomatoes and sprinkle with half the cheese. Season with salt and pepper. Repeat layers ending with remaining grated provolone. Bake, uncovered, about 30 minutes, until hot and light brown. Let stand 15 minutes. Remove springform pan and cut torte into wedges.

Serve to 8 Italian wannabes with mixed greens and garlic bread.

HONEY-BAKED CHICKEN AND SWEET POTATOES

French Dressing:

¹/₃ cup (75 mL) vegetable oil

2 Tbsp. (30 mL) white wine vinegar

¹/₂ tsp. (2 mL) paprika

¹/₄ tsp. (1 mL) dry mustard

¹/₄ tsp. (1 mL) dried tarragon

1 garlic clove, minced

¹/₃ cup (75 mL) liquid honey

salt and pepper to taste

8 boneless, skinless chicken breast halves

salt and pepper to taste

2 sweet potatoes, peeled and cut into bite-sized pieces

To make dressing, mix oil, vinegar, paprika, dry mustard, tarragon, garlic, honey, salt and pepper together.

———

Preheat oven to 350°F (180°C).

———

Sprinkle chicken with salt and pepper and place in deep casserole. Pour dressing over chicken; cover and bake for 30 minutes.

———

Boil potatoes just until fork tender. Drain. After chicken has cooked for 30 minutes, add sweet potatoes to casserole, stir to coat, cover and cook another 20 minutes.

———

Mmmmmm!
Serves 4-6.

CARAMELIZED ONION AND POTATO FLAN

2 Tbsp. (30 mL) **butter**

2 large onions, thinly sliced

6-8 medium baker potatoes, peeled and thinly sliced

salt and freshly ground pepper to taste

¹/₂-³/₄ lbs. (250-375 g) **Emmenthal or Gruyère cheese, grated**

In large frying pan over medium heat, sauté onions in butter until deep golden brown, about 20 minutes. Cook slowly to caramelize.

Grease a 9x13" (23x33 cm) or large round baking dish. Layer half the potato slices in a shingle fashion and season. Top with half the onions and Emmenthal. Repeat next layer, ending with cheese. Bake at 350°F (180°C) for 50 minutes, or until potatoes are fork tender. Cut in squares or wedges to serve.

This is one of the first recipes Chef Vincent shared with us – SOLD!
Excellent with ham or roast beef.
Serves 8.

COWBOY POT ROAST WITH YAMS AND JALAPEÑO KETCHUP

Jalapeño Ketchup:

3 jalapeño peppers, stemmed, seeded and diced

¹/₄ cup (60 mL) **minced onion**

2 garlic cloves, minced

1¹/₂ cups (375 mL) **water**

2 Tbsp. (30 mL) **brown sugar**

1¹/₂ tsp. (7 mL) **cumin**

4¹/₂ oz. (123 g) **tomato paste**

salt and freshly ground pepper

Pot Roast:

¹/₂ cup (125 mL) **flour**

1 tsp. (5 mL) **salt**

1 tsp. (5 mL) **freshly ground pepper**

4-6 lb. (2-3 kg) **chuck roast**

¹/₂ cup (125 mL) **vegetable oil**

3 carrots, peeled and cut in chunks

3 yams or sweet potatoes, peeled and cut into 2" (5 cm) **pieces**

1 medium onion, cut in quarters

4 garlic cloves, minced

2 cups (500 mL) **beef stock**

To make Jalapeño Ketchup, place peppers, onion, garlic and water in saucepan. Bring to boil over high heat and simmer for 15 minutes, or until peppers have absorbed some liquid and become soft. Remove pepper mixture with slotted spoon to food processor. Reserve liquid. To food processor, add brown sugar, cumin, tomato paste, salt, pepper and ¹/₄ cup (60 mL) reserved liquid. Purée, adding more pepper liquid, if needed, to reach desired thickness. Add salt and pepper and more brown sugar if desired.

Mix together flour, salt and pepper. Dredge roast in flour mixture.

Heat oil in large ovenproof pot. Sear roast for 4 minutes on each side, or until well browned.

Add Jalapeño Ketchup, carrots, yams, onion and garlic to pot. Cook 5 minutes. Add beef stock; cover and bring to boil. Place pot in 300°F (150°C) oven and cook for 2¹/₂ to 3 hours, or until beef is very tender.

Serve with homemade biscuits.

The best pot roast we've tasted in years. Yahoo! Serves 6-8.

PORK MEDALLIONS WITH MUSTARD SAUCE

2 lb. (1 kg) **pork tenderloin**

Marinade:

⅓ cup (75 mL) **red wine**

⅓ cup (75 mL) **chicken stock**

2 Tbsp. (30 mL) **Dijon mustard**

1 Tbsp. (15 mL) **fresh lemon juice**

1 Tbsp. (15 mL) **mustard seed**

2 garlic cloves, minced

1 tsp. (5 mL) **cumin**

2 tsp. (10 mL) **Worcestershire sauce**

¼ tsp. (1 mL) **salt**

freshly ground pepper

⅛ tsp. (0.5 mL) **red pepper flakes**

¼ cup (60 mL) **cold butter**

2 Tbsp. (30 mL) **chopped fresh chives**

Cut pork into 8 equal slices. Place slices in single layer in shallow baking dish.

In small bowl, mix together marinade ingredients.

Pour marinade over meat, cover and refrigerate for 2 hours. Remove pork slices from marinade and place on broiler pan. Pour marinade into small saucepan and bring to a boil over high heat. Boil marinade until reduced by half.

Turn heat down to low and swirl in butter a little at a time. Do not boil.

Preheat oven to broil. Broil pork slices 3 minutes per side. Transfer to plates, allowing 2 slices per person. Spoon a little sauce over pork and sprinkle with chives.

Serve with Whipped Potato with Celery Root on page 16.
Serves 4.

OUTRAGEOUS CHOCOLATE MARQUISE WITH RASPBERRY COULIS

Chocolate Sponge Base:

**3 large eggs,
room temperature**

1/2 cup (125 mL) **sugar**

1/3 cup (75 mL) **flour**

2 Tbsp. (30 mL) **cocoa powder**

2 Tbsp. (30 mL)
Kahlúa liqueur

Top Layer:

12 oz. (340 g) **semisweet
good quality chocolate
(e.g. Belgian, Swiss, Dutch)**

1 cup (250 mL) **butter**

1/3 cup (75 mL) **cocoa powder**

3/4 cup (175 mL) **coffee, warm**

4 large egg whites

1/2 cup (125 mL) **berry sugar**

Raspberry Coulis:

10 oz. pkg. (300 g)
**frozen raspberries, thawed
(save some for garnish)**

1/4 cup (60 mL) **sugar**

2 tsp. (10 mL) **fresh
lemon juice**

Beat eggs, add sugar and beat until well blended.

———

Preheat oven to 350°F (180°C). Sift flour and cocoa together and fold into egg mixture. Spread in lightly greased 9" (23 cm) springform pan. Bake for 15 minutes or until toothpick comes out clean. Cool.

———

Brush Kahlúa on cooled sponge cake.

———

In double boiler, melt chocolate and butter together.

———

Mix cocoa in coffee to dissolve. Blend into chocolate butter mixture.

———

Beat egg whites until stiff. Add sugar gradually at low speed. Gently fold whites into chocolate mixture. Pour over sponge cake base and refrigerate overnight.

———

To prepare Raspberry Coulis, place raspberries in saucepan. Add sugar and lemon juice and cook gently until sugar is dissolved. Strain through sieve and cool. Makes 2 cups (500 mL).

———

To serve, decorate each plate with dots of Raspberry Coulis, whole raspberries and Candied Orange Slices on page 126.

———

The name says it all! Can also be served with Sauce Anglaise on page 133. Serves 10-12.

CANDIED ORANGE SLICES

1 cup (250 mL) **water**

2 cups (500 mL) **sugar**

2 small oranges, sliced as thinly as possible

In saucepan, bring water and sugar to a boil. Cook until sugar has dissolved.

Layer orange slices in shallow frying pan. Add hot syrup and simmer for approximately 30 minutes. Remove from heat and let sit for 15 minutes. Remove orange slices from syrup and lay on parchment paper on cookie sheet. Dry in a 150-170°F (65-77°C) oven at least 3 hours. Slices should be crisp and translucent. Place slices between parchment paper and store in a sealed container.

Serve as a garnish on your favourite dessert.

A chefly garnish! Pictured on page 125.

LEMON OATMEAL CRUMBLE SQUARE

Crust:

²/₃ **cup** (150 mL) **butter**

1 **cup** (250 mL) **brown sugar**

1 **cup** (250 mL) **flour**

1 **tsp.** (5 mL) **baking powder**

¹/₄ **tsp.** (1 mL) **salt**

1 **cup** (250 mL) **rolled oats**

zest of 1 lemon, grated

juice of 2 lemons

10 **oz. can** (300 mL) **sweetened condensed milk**

Cream together butter and brown sugar. Add flour, baking powder, salt and rolled oats. Mix until crumbly. Press half the mixture into 9" (23 cm) square pan.

Combine lemon zest, juice and condensed milk and pour over crust. Sprinkle remaining crust mixture over top. Bake at 350°F (180°C) for 30 minutes or until edges are slightly browned.

Chill before serving. Freezes well.

LITTLE STICKY TOFFEE PUDDINGS

1 cup (250 mL) **water**

1/2 tsp. (2 mL) **vanilla**

1/2 tsp. (2 mL) **baking soda**

1 cup (250 mL)
dried cranberries

_____

3/4 cup (175 mL) **butter**

2/3 cup (150 mL) **sugar**

_____

2 eggs

_____

1 cup (250 mL) **flour**

1/4 tsp. (1 mL) **baking powder**

_____

Toffee Sauce:

1 cup (250 mL) **brown sugar**

1/2 cup (125 mL) **butter**

1/2 cup (125 mL)
whipping cream

_____

Butter 8, 1/2 cup (125 mL) ramekins. Bring water to a boil and add vanilla and baking soda, then add dried cranberries and set aside to cool.

_____

Cream butter and sugar until light and fluffy.

_____

Lightly beat eggs and gradually add to butter mixture in 3 stages.

_____

Sift flour and baking powder together and gently fold into batter. Fold cranberry mixture into batter. Portion into ramekins and bake at 350°F (180°C) for 25 minutes.

_____

To prepare Toffee Sauce, combine sauce ingredients in saucepan and stir over low heat until sugar is dissolved. Simmer until sauce thickens.

_____

To serve, remove puddings from ramekins by running a knife around edge. Invert on plate and drizzle with warm Toffee Sauce.

_____

Serves 8.

CHEF'S TIP

*The Toffee Sauce
is outstanding over vanilla
ice cream. Keep some on hand!*

LEMON SHORTBREAD COOKIES

³/₄ **cup** (175 mL) **butter, softened**

¹/₃ **cup** (75 mL) **icing sugar**

1 tsp. (5 mL) **grated lemon zest**

1 Tbsp. (15 mL) **fresh lemon juice**

1¹/₄ **cups** (310 mL) **flour**

¹/₂ **cup** (125 mL) **cornstarch**

Frosting:

³/₄ **cup** (175 mL) **icing sugar**

¹/₄ **cup** (60 mL) **butter, softened**

1 tsp. (5 mL) **grated lemon zest**

1 tsp. (5 mL) **fresh lemon juice**

In large bowl, cream butter and icing (confectioner's) sugar. Mix in lemon zest and juice.

Add flour and cornstarch and mix thoroughly.

Divide dough in half. Shape each half into a 1" (2.5 cm) roll.
Wrap in plastic wrap and refrigerate for at least 1 hour, or until ready to bake.

Preheat oven to 350°F (180°C). Using sharp knife, cut into ¹/₄" (1 cm) slices. Place each slice 2" (5 cm) apart on cookie sheet. Bake for 8-12 minutes, or until set. These cookies do not brown. Cool completely.

In small bowl combine icing (confectioner's) sugar, butter, lemon zest and lemon juice. Beat until light and fluffy.

Frost cooled cookies then hide them before the children discover your new best recipe!

The Christmas baking list just increased by one!
Makes 4 dozen.

CHOCOLATE CHOCOLATE CRANBERRY COOKIES

14 oz. (400 g) **semisweet chocolate, cut in chunks**

2 oz. (55 g) **unsweetened chocolate, cut in chunks**

¹/₂ cup (125 mL) **butter**

1 tsp. (5 mL) **instant espresso powder or instant coffee powder**

¹/₂ cup (125 mL) **flour**

¹/₂ tsp. (2 mL) **baking powder**

¹/₂ tsp. (2 mL) **salt**

3 large eggs

1 cup (250 mL) **sugar**

2 tsp. (10 mL) **vanilla**

1 cup (250 mL) **sliced almonds, toasted**

1 cup (250 mL) **semisweet chocolate chips**

1 cup (250 mL) **dried cranberries**

In top of double boiler combine chocolate, butter and coffee powder. Over low heat, stir until smooth and set aside to cool.

Mix flour, baking powder and salt together and set aside.

In large bowl, beat eggs, sugar and vanilla together until light and fluffy. Add cooled chocolate mixture and blend thoroughly. Fold in flour mixture.

Gently mix in almonds, chocolate chips and cranberries.

Using tablespoon, drop dough onto greased baking sheets and bake at 350°F (180°C) for 10 minutes.

Wickedly delicious! Makes about 3 dozen.

GINGER COOKIES

1¹/₂ **cups** (375 mL) **shortening**

2 **cups** (500 mL) **sugar**

2 **eggs, beaten**

¹/₄ **cup** (60 mL) **molasses**

4 **cups** (1 L) **flour**

4 **tsp.** (20 mL) **baking soda**

¹/₂ **tsp.** (2 mL) **salt**

4 **tsp.** (20 mL) **ground ginger**

2 **tsp.** (10 mL) **ground cinnamon**

2 **tsp.** (10 mL) **ground cloves**

¹/₄ **tsp.** (1 mL) **ground white pepper (optional)**

sugar

In large bowl, cream shortening and sugar together.

Beat eggs and molasses together and blend with creamed sugar mixture.

Combine flour, baking soda, salt, ginger, cinnamon, cloves and white pepper.

Add dry ingredients to creamed mixture and blend well. Chill for 1 hour.

Shape dough into 1" (1.5 cm) balls and roll in sugar.

Preheat oven to 350°F (180°C). Place balls on cookie sheets 2" (5 cm) apart and bake for 8-9 minutes.

Makes about 6 dozen spicy cookies! Pictured on page 95.

SAUCE ANGLAISE

4 egg yolks

1/3 cup (75 mL) **sugar**

1 cup (250 mL) **milk**

1 tsp. (5 mL) **vanilla**

Whisk yolks and sugar together in medium saucepan.

In small saucepan bring milk and vanilla to a boil, then whisk into egg yolk mixture. Return custard to stove over low heat. Stir continuously with wooden spoon, about 4 minutes. When sauce coats the back of a metal spoon, it is ready.

Do not allow sauce to boil or it will curdle. Makes 1 1/2 cups (375 mL).

Serve with Almond Plum Tart on page 90 and Outrageous Chocolate Marquise on page 124.

INDEX

THREE WAYS TO ORDER
THE BEST OF BRIDGE COOKBOOKS

Visit our website:
www.bestofbridge.com

Call our toll-free number:
1-800-883-4674

Write us:
**The Best of Bridge
Publishing Ltd.
6037-6th Street S.E.
Calgary, Alberta
T2H 1L8**

Telephone: (403) 252-0119
Fax: (403) 252-0206

A YEAR OF THE BEST

Seasonal Recipes from
The Best of Bridge with
Chef Vincent Parkinson
$27.95 (21.95 US)

**THE BEST OF
THE BEST**

Collection
of Favourites
Plus 70 New
Recipes

$24.95
(18.95 US)

**THE BEST
OF BRIDGE**

Royal
Treats For
Entertaining

$19.95
(14.95 US)

ENJOY!

More
Recipes
From
The Best
of Bridge

$19.95
(14.95 US)

WINNERS

More
Recipes
From
The Best
of Bridge

$19.95
(14.95 US)

GRAND SLAM

More
Recipes
From
The Best
of Bridge

$19.95
(14.95 US)

ACES

More
Recipes
From
The Best
of Bridge

$19.95
(14.95 US)

**THAT'S
TRUMP**

Featuring
Fat-Reduced
Recipes

$19.95
(14.95 US)

Shipping & Handling:
Canada & US Orders: *Add $6.00 for first copy, plus $1.00 for each additional copy.*
Add 7% G.S.T. (Canada only).
International Orders: *Add $15.00 US for first copy, plus $1.00 for each additional copy.*
Prices subject to change.